Granny Quilts

Vintage Quilts of the '30s
Made New for Today

Darlene Zimmerman

Published by

krause publications

700 East State Street • Iola, WI 54990-0001

Please call or write for our free catalog of publications. To place an order or obtain a free catalog, please call 800-258-0929. Please use our regular business telephone 715-445-2214 for further information or editorial comment.

Library of Congress Catalog Number: 2002107604
ISBN: 0-87349-501-2

Acknowledgments

It takes the cooperation of many people to put together a book such as this. I would like to thank the following people, for without their help, expertise, and encouragement, this book would not have happened!
My husband, for his encouragement and support.
Julie Stephani, my acquisition editor, and Christine Townsend, my editor, for all that they have done to make this book possible in such a short time period.
The book designer and photography staff at Krause for their fine work.
The design department at Wm. Wright Co. for providing the graphics for the tool tutorial.
Chanteclaire Fabrics, Inc. for their fabrics; A&E Thread Co. for providing thread; and Fairfield Corp. for supplying batting.
My sister, Lanie Tiffenbach, for the loan of her *Scrappy Baskets* quilt.
My daughter, Rachel Shelburne, for designing the basket in *Peek-a-Boo Baskets*, and her artwork on the *Friendship Butterfly* and *Lavender Ladies*.
Jeri Hillmeier for the loan of the *Friendship Butterfly* quilt.
Pam Kienholz for her lovely hand quilting on *Aunt Maggie's* quilt.
Bonnie Erickson for the wonderful machine quilting on the *Grandmother's Fan* quilt.
Gay Bomers for the loan of her sweet *Sunbonnet Sue* quilt.
Eleanor Levie, Joan Rockvoy, Pam Jacklitch, and others for their creativity in naming the quilts.
Cheryl Boyum for the loan of her crazy quilt.
Margy Manderfeld for sharing her binding technique.
Deb Jacobs and Kathy Squibb for their help in editing.
The anonymous makers of the vintage tops showcased in this book.

Dedication

This book is dedicated to the memory of my Granny – Emma Meta Matilda Meyer. My earliest memories are of her sewing, quilting, crocheting, tatting, cooking, or gardening. I loved her garden. She planted more flowers than vegetables … she always knew the names of the flowers, and could make anything grow. She would let me pick a beautiful bouquet each time we came to visit. Unfortunately, I didn't inherit her green thumb.

Grandma's hands were never idle. She was always working on some project or another: crocheting or tatting projects would be waiting to be picked up on a side table … there would be a stack of quilt pieces waiting to be sewn together on the treadle sewing machine in her spare bedroom … or the treadle machine sported a template, pencil, fabric, and scissors ready to cut more pieces. When it wasn't too cold or too hot in the attic, Grandma would put up the big quilting frame and begin quilting the tops she had finished piecing. If the weather turned too cold, she brought the quilt down to finish quilting in a hoop. I remember watching her quilt, and the number of tiny stitches that went into a quilt boggled my mind. How much love and patience was stitched into each quilt! I was fascinated by the whole process, and continue to be to this day. She made many quilts and gave a quilt to each of her 16 grandchildren.

When I attended college in the same town where my Grandma lived, I asked her to show me how to make a quilt. My mother had taught me how to sew, and even though I sewed most of my own fashions, I quickly learned that quilting is quite different from sewing clothes. And naturally, I picked the most beautiful quilt pattern I knew – *Grandmother's Flower Garden* – which is also one of the most difficult patterns to machine piece. In my spare time in college, I spent many hours tracing around a cardboard template and cutting the pieces by hand.

Marriage after college, several years of teaching school, and starting a family all sidetracked me from quilting for a few years. By the time I was ready to take it up again (by this time a stay-at-home mom with three pre-schoolers), my Grandma had passed away. I had to teach myself how to put those hexagons together. My mother advised me to wait until I was older and my kids were grown before I took up quilting for a hobby – but watching Georgia Bonesteel on television and learning about "lap quilting" convinced me I *could* do it now. I did finally put together those hexagons (by hand) and made two twin-sized quilts for my daughters. From there, I went on to make many more quilts, design quilting tools, write books, and design fabrics. Grandma, I am sure, is looking down from heaven with approval (and probably a lot of astonishment). Grandma, thanks for inspiring me. I still miss you!

Table of Contents

Introduction

The '30s quilts – how we love them! If you aren't lucky enough to own a family heirloom or have enough "pin money" to purchase one of these vintage beauties, you can make your own using the directions in this book. The first section, entitled "What Makes a '30s Quilt," is a short history lesson on color and design, and how it relates to quiltmaking in the past 150 years in this country, and goes on to explore some of the characteristics of a '30s-era quilt.

The next section, entitled "How to Make a '30s Quilt," will give you some definite direction on how to go about choosing fabric, setting the blocks, quilting, and finishing the edges in the manner of a '30s quilt, while at the same time using modern rotary cutting methods and time-saving techniques.

Please familiarize yourself with the suggested tools listed for each pattern. A tool tutorial is given on pages 124-128. I prefer to use the tools for ease and accuracy, but alternate cutting directions for most of the shapes are given if you choose not to use the tools. Note that different size strips will need to be cut if not using the tools.

The quilts shown in this book are primarily designed to fit beds. However, beds come in different sizes, and the new extra-thick mattresses make it difficult to write a one-size-fits-all pattern. Also, some people prefer the bed-quilt to be used as a bedspread, and want it to drape to the floor. Others prefer the quilt to overhang only a few inches. Before you begin a project, measure the bed the quilt is destined for to determine the size quilt *you* want to make. Compare this to the finished sizes given for the project, and make adjustments either in the number of blocks or the width of the sashes or borders. For most of the projects, two sizes are listed, with the smaller size given first, the larger size in parentheses. Once you have chosen the size you want to make, highlight the numbers you need to prevent any mix-ups in cutting.

Think of the projects in this book as a starting point for your inspiration. Feel free to add your own interpretation to the designs. Deviate from the color choices presented – add your own flair! We don't need to make exact copies of the vintage quilts; we can add a bit of the current era (and our own personality) to our creations.

In this introduction, I would like to add just a few words of wisdom: Enjoy the process! While neatness and accuracy are important, allow your quilt to be less than perfect. The vintage (and new) quilts in this book are not perfect and, quite often, the little imperfections are what give the quilt its character and charm. The *Primrose Basket* (page 95) quilt is a perfect example. If you were to look closely, you would see many of the points were cut off to make the blocks the same size. Does it affect how you view the quilt? No, it is still charming. Confetti (page 105) is another example. The original quiltmaker didn't have an accu-

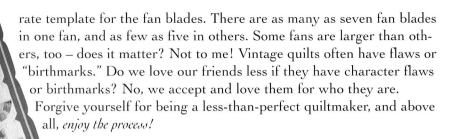

rate template for the fan blades. There are as many as seven fan blades in one fan, and as few as five in others. Some fans are larger than others, too – does it matter? Not to me! Vintage quilts often have flaws or "birthmarks." Do we love our friends less if they have character flaws or birthmarks? No, we accept and love them for who they are. Forgive yourself for being a less-than-perfect quiltmaker, and above all, *enjoy the process!*

What Makes a '30s Quilt?

Quilts made in the era from about 1920 to 1950 have a distinctive look; they are different from the quilts that were made before that time, and different from those that came after. Generally referred to as "'30s quilts," the style these quilts embraced spanned a period of about 30 years, but it is only in the past few years that they have they become recognized as belonging to that particular era, and have once again become popular.

For many, the quilts from this era remind us of our mothers, or of our grandmothers or aunts. Others who aren't fortunate enough to have a quilting heritage may simply enjoy '30s quilts for their pretty and cheerful color schemes and distinctive patterns and styles.

The Color Factor in Vintage Quilts

Most vintage quilts are anonymous – no names or dates are inscribed upon them, so that the stories behind the quilt, and even the origins of the quilt, are lost. As a result, quilt historians have to use clues from the quilt fabrics (the colors and the designs in the prints) to help them place a vintage quilt in a particular era.

The colors are what make '30s quilts so distinctive. These quilts were generally pastel in color, bearing a wide range of small-scale, multi-colored pastel prints or solids on a white, or off-white, background … although sometimes, a few dark blue indigo prints, mourning grays, or Turkey red patches from an earlier era appeared, having been dredged up from a deep scrap-bag.

Quiltmakers use the fabric scraps they have on hand or can purchase, and for the quilters in the times before the '30s, the colors of these fabric pieces were generally quite dark – for good reason. Up until the 1920s, all fabric dyes were vegetable-based, and were not very colorfast. Pastel colors were just too difficult to obtain with vegetable dyes. And, in the days before automatic washing machines and laundry detergents, the standards of cleanliness were not what they are now. Imagine having only one or two changes of clothes, taking a bath on Saturday night in the wash tub (whether it was wanted or not), and the family wash being done once a month! In times like those, dark clothing was *definitely* an asset.

Many fabrics would start out being a particular color but fade with age (or turn another color altogether). The old green fabrics were particularly noted for this, which is why you sometimes see a lovely appliquéd quilt with red flowers blooming from *tan* stems and leaves – certainly not what the original quiltmaker intended!

Quilters from these times wanted to use the most colorfast dyes possible, and relied on those that were tried and true: indigo (dark blue), Turkey red (dyed by a long, involved process developed in Turkey), madders (rusty reds and oranges), double pinks, and antimony orange. Such colors, it need not be said, naturally made for rather dark quilts.

Quilt History

Before the turn of the last century, mourning grays (black lines or dots on a white ground that appeared gray), burgundy reds, indigo blues, and shirting prints (prints with tiny designs in black or red on a white ground) became popular choices for quiltmaking and are distinctive to the time period from 1875 to 1900.

After 1900, the "old-fashioned" quilt went out of style, and was replaced with the "crazy quilt." These weren't quilts meant for a bed, but rather were meant to be displayed in a Victorian parlor – they were status symbols announcing to the world that the woman of the house had enough money to purchase such luxury fabrics, and the leisure time to spend embroidering on them. Crazy quilts were made of irregularly shaped, heavily embroidered patches of velvet, silk, and satin, covered with laboriously stitched designs and elaborate embellishments – some of the patches were even painted. Old-time quiltmakers said if you weren't crazy when you started one, you were crazy when you finished one! Heavily promoted by magazines and department stores, the crazy

Cotton crazy quilt, circa 1920-40.

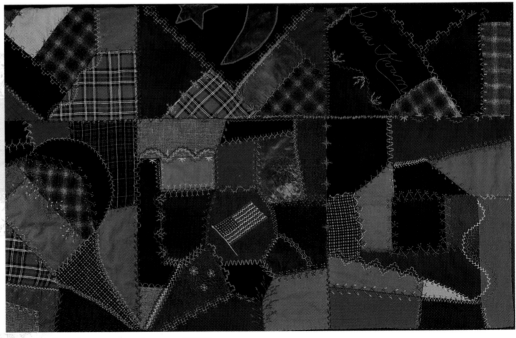

Wool, silk, velvet crazy quilt, circa 1900s.

quilt became all the rage, dovetailing the Victorian love of embellishment and sentimentality. Crazy quilts often contained names, dates, and souvenir ribbons from political parties, and mementos of important events or places. In the '30s, the crazy quilt was sometimes translated into cotton fabrics for a completely different look. Even today the crazy quilt continues to be popular among quiltmakers.

So what happened to bring back the popularity of traditional, pieced cotton quilts and to make the quilts from the '30s era so distinctive? Sadly, war and hard times produced the circumstances from which these lovely quilts evolved. Up until WW I, Germany was the developer of fabric dyes, but they became impossible to obtain during WW I, so we, in the United States, developed our own dyes based on new petroleum products. These new dyes were colorfast, relatively easy to use – and *pastel*. The "new" colors that became so popular for quiltmakers were lavender, "that" green, butter yellow, sky blue, pink, peach, tangerine (orange), and red. The colors shown here are actual vintage solid color swatches. There was no one *exact* color of green, pink, yellow, etc., but rather a range of these clear, pastel colors.

The United States government also promoted quiltmaking with its slogan: "Make quilts, save the blankets for the boys over there!" Newspapers, women's magazines, and department stores all promoted quiltmaking by providing patterns and kits. Mountain Mist batting company began putting quilting patterns on the inside of the batting wrappers. This was the first time that women were able to readily purchase quilting patterns. Before this time, women copied patterns off of quilts belonging to friends and relatives. Now, a whole range of new patterns became available to them. Some of the new patterns that emerged during this time that are synonymous with the '30s era are: *Grandmother's Flower Garden* (page 110), *Dresden Plate* (page 120), *Double Wedding Ring*, *Sunbonnet Sue*, *Grandmother's Fan* (page 90), and *Job's Tears* (page 76). Both finished and unfinished quilts in these patterns can still be found today. Some of the patterns (*Double Wedding Ring, Dresden Plate, Grandmother's Fan,* and *Sunbonnet Sue*) were developed during this era. Others (*Grandmother's Flower Garden* and *Job's Tears*) were adapted from older patterns.

These mail-order or newspaper patterns were not like the patterns we purchase today with clear, step-by-step instructions illustrated with graphics, although templates were always given (which may or may not have been accurate). The quiltmaker was directed to piece a certain number of blocks, general directions were given on how to set them together either directly, with alternate blocks, or with sashing, then directed to border, quilt and bind. Very little instruction was given on any of the many steps involved, as some level of familiarity with quilt-making was apparently assumed. But, while quiltmaking was very popular, not everyone had learned to make quilts from their grandmothers, aunts or mothers — and many of the popular patterns were not easy to piece; so, between the difficulty factor and the inexperience of some quiltmakers, some vintage quilt tops were never finished! Even today, with all our modern tools and equipment, most quilters hesitate to even attempt a *Double Wedding Ring* with all the curved seams.

Most quilters in the past pieced their quilts by hand, or used a combination of hand and machine piecing. Generally, the machine work was saved for the sashing seams and the long border seams. The intricate work was pieced by hand. Even as few as 20 years ago there was a debate raging as to whether or not a quilt was "real" if it was pieced by machine! While I admire the quiltmakers of the past for their dedication in cutting and piecing by hand, I certainly wouldn't trade my rotary cutter, sewing machine, or tools for a trip down Memory Lane. These were practical women and, in my opinion, would have jumped at the chance to use any labor-saving devices.

Kit Quilts

Ruby McKim, a quilt designer from the 1930s era, sold patterns as well as pre-cut kits for pieced and appliquéd quilts. An old *Patchwork Patterns #631,* a booklet from the McKim Studios (circa 1930s) gives twelve quilt patterns and offers ready-cut quilt kits for a number of the patterns. A *Blazing Star* quilt kit was $4.75, an *Irish Chain* quilt kit was $4.00, and a *Rose of Sharon* quilt kit cost $7.00. Perforated quilting patterns for each of the designs were also available for 20 cents.

Kit quilts from other companies were also available to women through mail order or department stores. These kits contained everything needed to make the quilt top, and sometimes also included the backing and binding. Usually these quilts were designed by anonymous artists and most often were appliquéd, not pieced. Most used only solid colors, but a few used prints as well. Many of them can be challenging to appliqué, and usually have at least some embroidery details. The quilt design was stamped on the background fabric, and each piece was coded. Various shapes from the design were stamped on colored fabric (usually solid) and also coded. So, if you cut out a green leaf #G-4, you found the corresponding number on the background and appliquéd it in place. Embroidery details could also be added.

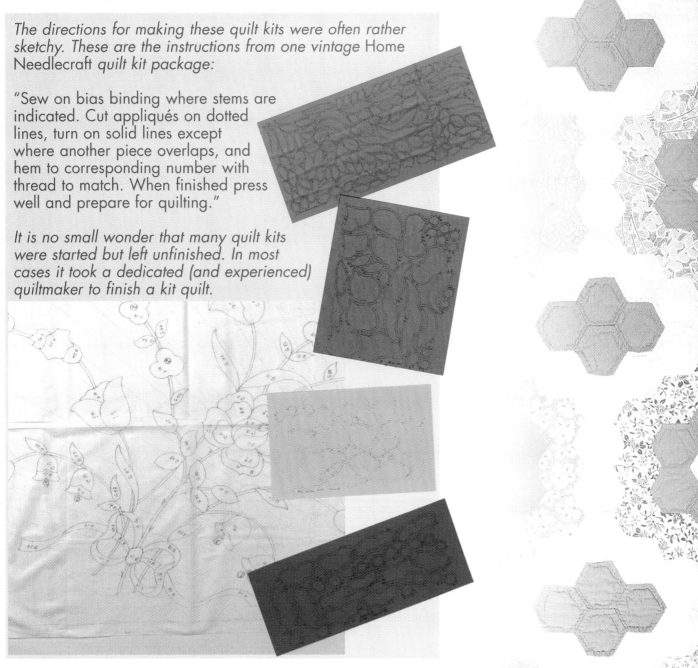

The directions for making these quilt kits were often rather sketchy. These are the instructions from one vintage Home Needlecraft *quilt kit package:*

"Sew on bias binding where stems are indicated. Cut appliqués on dotted lines, turn on solid lines except where another piece overlaps, and hem to corresponding number with thread to match. When finished press well and prepare for quilting."

It is no small wonder that many quilt kits were started but left unfinished. In most cases it took a dedicated (and experienced) quiltmaker to finish a kit quilt.

Scrap Quilts

Another feature of '30s quilts is the wide variety of scraps employed. While quilts have always been made from leftover dressmaking goods, the '30s quilts show a broader range of fabrics and colors. Some of this may be due to the increased size of wardrobes in the 1900s, and the variety and relatively low price of fabrics available to the home-maker.

Nearly everyone sewed their own clothes, or hired someone to sew for them. Most clothing was made from 100 percent cotton fabrics in the lovely pastel multicolored prints we see in the quilts from that era. Not only women's housedresses, but their aprons and the children's clothing were made from those fabrics, giving the homemaker quite a number of remnants to be used in quiltmaking. Garment factories sold their fabric scraps for a nominal price, which women also used for their quiltmaking.

The popular patterns from that time – *Grandmother's Flower Garden, Dresden Plate,* and *Double Wedding Ring* – were designs that allowed every bit of fabric to be used. Stringent economy on all fronts was praised as a virtue. "Making do or doing without" was not just a slogan. The women from this era *lived* by that code, and took pride in their frugality.

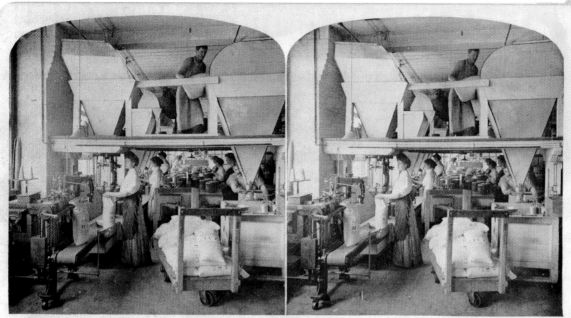

No. **7** AUTOMATIC MACHINES IN THE GROCERY DEPARTMENT.
SEARS, ROEBUCK & CO., Chicago, Ill.

Feedsacks

One can hardly talk about quilts or fabrics from the '30s without mentioning feedsacks and the role they played in quiltmaking. It's hard for us to imagine a time when foodstuffs were packaged in fabric bags instead of cardboard or plastic. Around the 1850s, cotton bags began replacing kegs and barrels for packaging. Up until the 1920s or 1930s, these bags were white, brown, or other solid colors. Naturally, homemakers would re-use these bags – bleach out the brand logo and recycle them into household linens, clothing, or quilts. Many of the white and off-white backgrounds you see in old quilts were probably once feedsacks.

Somewhere in the '20s or '30s, bag manufacturers began to make the printed cotton bags. There were different sizes and even different weaves. The finest weaves (and smaller bags) were for sugar or cornmeal. Flour came in 50# or 100# bags, and would also be a finer weave. Chicken feed would also be in 50# or 100# bags, but the weave was generally coarser. Every homemaker, whether she lived on a farm or not, had these bags. In those days everyone had to make their own bread and cooked from scratch, so a steady supply of these bags was coming into the home. The farm wife usually raised chickens, and often sold the chickens and eggs for a little extra household money. The sacks containing the chicken feed (sometimes referred to as "chicken

linen") were an extra bonus. The printed bags were so common and so available, that nearly everyone was wearing clothing made from them. These were hard times; the cotton feedsack fabric was often indistinguishable from purchased fabric, so there was no stigma attached to wearing homemade clothes made from feedsacks. Anna Lu Cook, author of *Identification and Value Guide to Textile Bags* says that in 1942, about 50 *million* print flour and feedbags were manufactured and sold. In 1942, one mill alone was making printed feedsacks in 1,000 different designs.

The scraps left from making clothing out of these feedsacks were also used in quiltmaking. It is not unusual to find quilt backs pieced from matching (or un-matched) feedsacks. Sometimes the coarser fabrics in a quilt can be identified as feedsacks, but a surprising number of sacks were made from a high-quality fabric and are indistinguishable from purchased dress goods. The only sure way of proving a fabric comes from a feedsack is finding the telltale holes along an edge left by the string that was used to sew the bags together.

Generally speaking, the smaller designs and pastel colors denote early feedsacks, and the larger, bolder prints indicate later feedsacks. By the end of the 1940s, cotton feedsacks were replaced by the much cheaper paper bags. Because of the huge numbers produced in the 20-30 year time span, it is still possible to find feedsacks today, and some quiltmakers enjoy collecting an endless variety and using them in their new quilts, or for restoration of old beauties. Some of the new reproduction '30s fabrics are copied from old feedsacks.

Use of Solid Fabrics

In '30s quilts, you see solid color fabrics in those lovely pastel colors used as accents, as sashes or borders, or used alone in conjunction with white (as seen in the kit quilts). Quilts made up of only the small, multicolored '30s prints can be quite "busy." In fact, if all the design elements are prints, the pattern is indistinguishable.

To showcase the print fabrics and to add a unifying element, white or a solid color fabric is often used as a background. The solids can also be used for accent – as important elements in the block, as sashings to separate the busy blocks, or as unifying elements in a quilt (see quilts on pages 26, 36, and 52 for examples on effective use of solids with prints).

Border and Binding Treatments

Thanks in part to quilts like *Double Wedding Ring* and *Grandmother's Flower Garden*, we began to see novel ways to finish the edges of quilts. These two patterns have irregular edges (and you will occasionally find *Grandmother's Flower Garden* quilts all finished except for the edges; it was apparent that some quiltmakers were stumped about binding that irregular edge). This particular design may be the origin for the scalloped edges we often see on '30s quilts. The kit quilt designers, and other professional quilt designers, used scalloped or shaped edges to continue or enhance the pieced or appliquéd design. The shaped-edge treatment may also have been influenced by the art-deco designs so popular at that time. A scalloped or shaped edge certainly takes an ordinary quilt and makes it *extra*-ordinary!

How to Make a '30s Quilt

Choosing Fabric

If you study the '30s-era vintage quilts presented in this book, as well as others that you have seen, you will notice they generally have a large number of small-to-medium scale prints in a variety of pastel colors. The pastel colors are *clear* colors, not the grayed tones of the 1890s, or the sepia-colored tones that are popular in the "primitive" look. Often the prints are set on white or off-white plain backgrounds, or occasionally on a solid-colored background. The quiltmakers of the time were using what they had on hand – the remnants from sewing house-dresses, children's clothing, and the ubiquitous household aprons. The white background fabric was often from bleached flour or feedsacks. Sometimes solids would be purchased and used as accents in the quilt, sashings, borders, or occasionally, backgrounds.

If you want to re-create the look of vintage quilts, you need a *variety* rather than a *quantity* of the print fabrics for the projects. For those of you who avidly collect '30s reproduction prints, this should not be a problem! However, if you are new to quiltmaking, you will want to seek out those clear pastels in small- or medium-scale prints. You can purchase small amounts of each – fat quarters or regular yardage. The patterns in this book suggest the total yardage needed for the prints, but try to have at least 10 different prints for the best variety – more is better in this case! Note the occasional red and dark blue mixed in with the pastel colors. Used judiciously, the darker colors can add some zip to the quilt, like adding raisins to bread pudding.

Use a variety of colors, as well. Don't worry about putting blue next to green, or pink next to red; they all look great together when used in small amounts. Choose the prints you like, and for a bit of fun, toss in a few novelty (animal, people, etc.) prints.

For background fabric, choose a white, off-white, or pastel color. I prefer using a slightly off-white (called *Vintage White* by Chanteclaire Fabrics, Inc.), as it matches the background in the prints and looks almost antique, but not dirty or yellowed.

If you have a collection of feedsacks or some remnants from your grandmother's sewing basket, you can incorporate those fabrics in your quilts. You'll notice, when buying (and cutting) vintage fabrics, that they only measure about 36" wide instead of 42".

If you choose, pre-wash the fabric for your project in lukewarm water, dry, and press it before using. A little spray starch works wonders on limp fabric.

Choosing a Design

Before purchasing fabric for a project, be sure to read through your pattern directions in order to understand the steps involved. The number of pieces in each block and the shape of the pieces determine the difficulty involved. But remember, any project you undertake, no matter how large or complicated, is not impossible if you take it *one step at a time*.

Before cutting out all the pieces, take the time to make a sample block or unit to see if you like how the fabrics and colors work together. You can easily make adjustments at this point. With the variety of prints you are using, you can either arrange them randomly, or deliberately choose the placement of each piece and repeat it exactly in each block; choose the method that works best for you!

Cutting

In each of the patterns in this book, all the larger pieces of fabric are cut the *width* of the fabric (selvage to selvage), unless you choose to cut the borders lengthwise before you begin. Personally, I prefer to decide on borders after the quilt top is finished, then preview different possibilities, and different widths. There isn't a set formula for determining perfect borders in advance!

The Cutting Table shows the fabric to be cut in the first column. The second column lists the number and size of the strip(s) to be cut. The last column tells you the number and shape of the pieces to cut from those strips. *Seam allowances are included in those shapes.* The tool used to cut those pieces will also be noted. *Important: It is necessary to use the proper tool to cut the shapes.* **The tools are not interchangeable.** If you choose not to use the tools listed, alternate cutting directions are given below the cutting tables.

A Tool Tutorial is given on pages 124-128. Familiarize yourself with the tools before using them in a project. While all of them are *easy* to use, they should be used *correctly* for best results. The tools used in this book are intended to be all-purpose tools. Once you learn how to use them, you can adapt them for use in all your quiltmaking.

For most, if not all of the patterns, you will want a nice variety of prints in the blocks. For the print fabrics, the pattern generally lists the strip *size* first, then the number of pieces to cut from a *variety* of prints. The number of strips to cut is not always given, so you can use a wide variety of short strips or scraps to cut these pieces.

Cutting Accurately

Accurately-cut pieces mean fewer problems when sewing and fitting the pieces together, and will produce a quilt you can be proud of. Here are a few tips to make your cutting more accurate:

❖ Cut in natural light if at all possible.
❖ Put a new blade in your rotary cutter.
❖ Use a mat smoother or treat yourself to a new mat.
❖ Cut with the majority of the fabric toward your dominant hand (from left to right if you are right-handed, reverse if you are left-handed).
❖ Cut only two layers at a time. Cutting more layers may save you time, but the accuracy of the pieces will definitely suffer.
❖ Intersperse the cutting with the sewing and pressing. It's not good for your back to work longer than 20 minutes at any one task.

To keep everything organized once you're done cutting, label the pieces or strips. Place pieces in baggies, use sticky notes, or put them on paper plates (that you can also write on and stack).

Block Assembly

Quarter-inch seams are used throughout. The seam allowances are included in the cutting process, so it is important to sew *exact* ¼" seams. Use a ¼" foot for your sewing machine if at all possible, or mark the seam allowance with masking tape. You can determine where to mark on your sewing machine by putting the needle down on the ¼" line on one of your rotary cutting rulers. Set the presser foot down on the ruler and place masking tape next to the ruler to mark the ¼" (making sure not to cover the feed dogs).

To check that your seam allowance is correct, try this test: Cut three 1½" x 3½" strips. Sew them together on the long edges. Press. The square should be exactly 3½". If not, adjust your seam allowance and/or pressing technique.

Step-by-step instructions with graphics are given for each of the projects. Note there are pressing arrows or directions given on how the pieces should be pressed so the seams alternate. If no pressing directions are given, then press toward the darker fabric, or whichever side has the fewest seams.

Proper pressing is so important! The seams need to be pressed to one side without a pleat on the front side. Press the seam first just as it comes out of the machine, and then turn back the fabric you are pressing toward, and press the seam to one side. Press from the top side and keep the unit flat on the ironing board (don't pull up on it while pressing). Steam can be used when pressing the units, or after the block is completed.

To press strip sets (long strips of different fabrics sewn together), finger press the seams to one side before ironing. Then, place the strip set across the width (the short part) of the ironing board and press. Keep the strip set straight while ironing. Avoid curving the strip set, as that will distort the units cut from it.

The patterns give the measurements for the unfinished size of the units and blocks. This can help keep you on track. However, note that it is more important that the blocks all finish to the *same size* rather than be the exact size given in the pattern. Adjustments can be made to the sashings and borders to accommodate any slight differences.

Appliqué Techniques

Several of the projects in the book employ appliqué techniques, so several methods of appliqué are given here, but you can choose *your* favorite method.

Freezer Paper Appliqué

The templates for the projects are given with the patterns. Trace the shapes the number of times indicated in the pattern on the dull side of the freezer paper. (Note that you can re-use the shapes several times.) The templates are reversed in the book for tracing purposes. The patterns will match the quilts in the book when the appliqué is completed.

Cut out the shapes on the lines. Iron to the *wrong* side of the fabrics you have chosen for the appliqués, leaving at least ½" between the shapes. Cut out the shapes adding a scant ¼" seam allowance. Clip any inside corners. To make appliquéing easier, you can finger-press the edges of the fabric around the freezer paper or, with a warm iron, press the seam allowance over the edge of the freezer paper. Once the edge is well pressed, you can pull off the freezer paper and give it a last pressing. Now, it is a simple matter to blind stitch the shapes in place by hand with matching thread and a thin (sharps or straw) needle. Note that you will need to layer the shapes in the proper order. You may choose to do a blind hem stitch or a small zigzag with matching thread on your sewing machine. If you prefer a more decorative stitch, use black thread (on the sewing machine) and buttonhole stitch the shapes in place (by hand, use #8 pearl cotton in black). Or, yet another option would be to use the pearl cotton and hand stitch a running stitch close to the finished edge of the appliqué pieces. (See *Sunbonnet Sue* page 117).

Fusible Appliqué

Trace the shapes on the paper side of the fusible webbing. Cut out the shapes roughly. To eliminate some of the stiffness, cut out the centers of the shapes so only the edges are fused down.

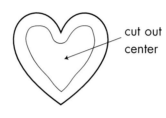

cut out center

Following manufacturer's directions, fuse the shapes to the wrong side of the fabrics chosen for the appliqué. Cut out on the drawn line (no need to add seam allowances). Fuse in place, layering as necessary. If this quilt will be used heavily and washed, the edges should also be machine stitched – either with a zigzag, a blind hem stitch, or buttonhole stitch.

Adding Borders

Borders are the frame for the quilt, and should enhance the quilt. Border width and fabric selections are given for each of the projects, but use them simply as starting points. Experiment with different widths, particularly if you want to change the size of the quilt. Try different fabrics – either different prints or a solid for a print or vice versa. See which combination of fabrics and widths works best for *your* quilt.

A painless way of determining the proper length for the border strips is to use the border strips to "measure" the quilt top instead of a measuring tape. Layer the top and bottom borders aligned with the left edge of the quilt top (away from the edge, as it may have stretched). Smooth out the borders across the width of the quilt. Fold and crease the border lengths at the right edge of the quilt. Cut the border lengths about 1" longer for insurance. Match the center of the border to the center of the quilt edge. Pin the border to the quilt top. Stitch, then trim off the excess length. Repeat for the bottom border. Press the seams toward the border.

Repeat this procedure for the sides of the quilt.

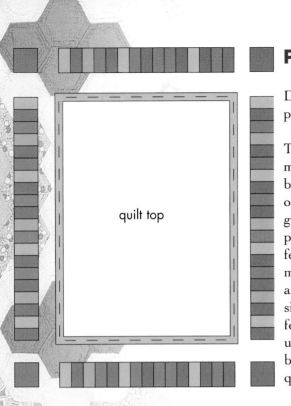

Pieced Borders

Several of the projects in the book have pieced borders. Don't panic! If you have avoided adding pieced borders in the past, try this easy method for making them fit.

Note that a plain border precedes all the pieced borders. Think of this plain border as a *spacing border*. You can easily make adjustments to this spacing border to make the pieced border fit properly; here's how: Cut the spacing border an inch or so wider than needed. Sew to the quilt in the manner suggested above. Also, assemble the pieced borders. Using the top pieced border, measure the *width* of the quilt. Measure the difference. Trim the *sides* of the quilt equally to equal the same measurement as the pieced borders. **Before** sewing on the top and bottom borders, measure the *length* of the quilt with the side pieced borders (excluding the corners). Measure the difference. Trim off equally any excess length. Add the corner units to the side borders. Now, you can sew on the top- and bottom-pieced borders, then the side-pieced borders to the quilt, and they will fit perfectly!

Mitered Borders

Measure and cut borders the width (or length) of the quilt plus border width times two, plus several more inches for insurance. Sew all four borders to the quilt top, centering the borders and stitching only to ¼" from the corners. Stop and backstitch. Press the seam allowances toward the quilt.

Hint: Multiple borders can be sewn together and treated like a single border when mitering the corners.

Fold the quilt on the diagonal, right sides together, matching raw edges, and having the borders extending outward.

Lay the Companion Angle (or a ruler) on your quilt with the longest edge on the diagonal fold, and the side of the tool aligned with the raw edges of the borders. Draw a line from the diagonal fold to the edge of the borders.

Pin the borders together along this line. Stitch on the line, backstitching at the inside corner.

Check the seam on the right side. If it is properly sewn, trim the seam to ¼" and press open.

Repeat for all four corners.

The Quilt Sandwich

After the quilt top is finished and has been given a final pressing, you may need to mark any quilting designs before layering. Some quilting techniques and marking devices lend themselves better to marking as you quilt, while others need to be marked before layering. Whatever marking tool or device you choose, test it on scraps from your project to see if the marks can be easily removed once the quilting is finished. *Always mark as lightly and as little as possible.*

Cut the batting and backing at least 4" larger than the quilt top (more if you are having it machine quilted on the professional quilting machine). If you want a traditional look, use a thin cotton batting. If you are hand quilting, I recommend using the cotton batting on a smaller project or sample to get a feel for it; it may be more difficult to needle. There are also thin polyester batts that will yield a similar, traditional look but are easier to needle.

Baste the three layers together every 4" either with safety pins or basting stitches. Before beginning the quilting, it is a good idea to turn the backing and batting up over the raw edges of the quilt and pin or baste them in place to keep the quilt top edges from raveling.

Quilting

Quilting suggestions are given for each of the projects in the book. Keep in mind these are only suggestions; feel free to choose your own method of quilting and your own designs.

Quilts from the '30s era were often quilted "by the piece" – that is, outlined ¼" from the seam lines. This is easy to do without marking. Larger areas will need more quilting to divide up the space. Try to balance the quilting; stitch about the same amount throughout the quilt. If quilting by machine, a small machine meander in the background can give the illusion of a slightly puckered, well-loved quilt.

A combination of hand and machine quilting can also be used. Showcase the hand quilting and use machine quilting where it's not as noticeable.

Binding

When the quilting is completed, machine baste (with a walking foot) or hand baste the edges a scant ¼" from the edge. This will hold the edges together and keep them from shifting while the binding is being sewn on.

Cut the binding strips 2¼" wide for double binding, 1¼" for single binding. You can use either bias or straight-of-grain strips for binding, whichever you prefer. The binding strips are joined with diagonal seams pressed open. For a double binding, press the binding strips in half, wrong sides together. For scalloped or

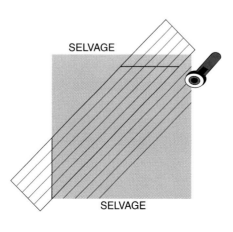

SELVAGE

SELVAGE

shaped edges, a single-fold *bias* binding is a must to help you get around those curves. To cut bias strips, align the 45-degree line on your long ruler with the selvage and cut diagonal strips. Join with diagonal seams pressed open. (See diagram on page 21.)

Sew the binding to the quilt with a ¼" seam, mitering the corners. To miter the corner, stitch to within a ¼" of the corner, and backstitch. Take the quilt out from under the presser foot and turn the quilt to begin stitching the next side. Pull the binding straight up, and then fold it at the edge of the quilt. Align the binding to the next edge of the quilt, and begin stitching at the fold. Repeat in this manner around the quilt.

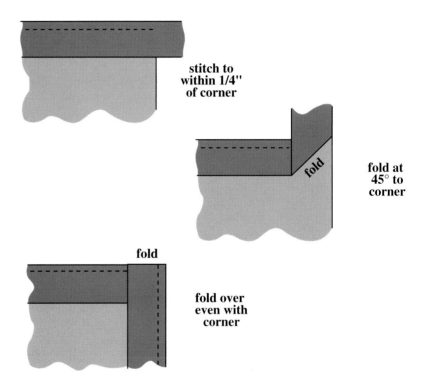

stitch to
within 1/4"
of corner

fold

fold at
45° to
corner

fold

fold over
even with
corner

Joining the Binding Ends

To join the binding ends with a no-lump ending, try this method: When you begin stitching the binding, start in the middle of one of the sides, leaving an 8" tail. Stitch the binding on all sides of the quilt, but stop about 10" from where you began. Remove the quilt from the machine.

10"

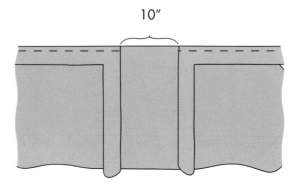

On a flat surface, pull the binding ends together to meet in the middle of that 10" space. Crease both ends where they meet, leaving a ¼" space between the ends. Cut one end off at the crease. Measure and cut the second end the *binding width* from the crease.

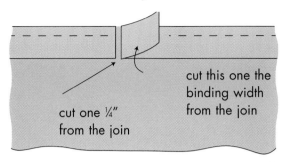

cut this one the binding width from the join

cut one ¼" from the join

Now join the two ends with a diagonal seam pressed open.

Finish sewing the binding to the quilt.

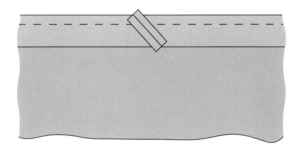

Quilt Labels

Sadly, many of the beautiful quilts from the past are anonymous. Even when a quilt has been passed down in the family, sometimes the significant information, such as who actually made it, and when and why, is lost. It is so important to label your quilt when it is finished. This is your legacy! The label should include:

❖For whom the quilt is intended
❖Who assembled and quilted it
❖When it was completed
❖Where it was made (city, town, country)
❖For what special occasion

A quilt label doesn't have to be fancy. It can be a simple square of muslin or fabric from the quilt that contains the necessary information written in permanent fabric ink. You can also purchase lovely quilt labels singly or by the yard. Sew or appliqué them to the back of the quilt when finished, or to the backing before layering. You can also sign the quilt on the front side (like artists do!) in some open area.

Storage

Whether a quilt is newly created or a vintage family heirloom, it deserves to be treated with respect. Even the vintage family heirlooms can be used or displayed if handled properly. Quilts are like people – they don't like extreme heat, cold, or damp. When not in use, keep them in a dark place wrapped in a well-used sheet or pillowcase. Plastic will trap moisture and bugs. Keep quilts from direct contact with paper or wood, as these contain acids that will stain and deteriorate the quilt fabrics.

When used or displayed, keep quilts out of direct sunlight. Even indirect sunlight will fade a quilt over time. Protect your quilts from misuse by pets or young children, but also enjoy their soft comforts. Quilts are meant to be used and enjoyed, but you can do so gently.

Washing a Quilt

When it is absolutely necessary to wash a quilt (sometimes all they need is airing), do so with a gentle detergent made specifically for washing quilts. Dissolve the detergent in lukewarm water before adding the quilt. You can use your washing machine for soaking and agitating by hand. The washing machine can also spin the water out of the quilt. Rinse thoroughly to remove any detergent.

As for stains, avoid using any harsh chemicals or bleach. Too many quilts have been ruined by good intentions and injudicious use of stain removers! Instead, try soaking in Oxy-Clean® or Biz® for 24 hours or more. These are enzyme soaks, and work slowly, but well. Be patient; give them enough time to work. Try not to agonize over a few light stains or spots – they can add character to a quilt!

Instead of using the dryer, lay the quilt on a bed, the floor, or even on a clean sheet outdoors. Position a fan to blow over the quilt to speed the drying process. When one side is completely dry, turn it over to dry the second side. Wait until thoroughly dry before folding or storing.

With loving care, your quilts will become treasured heirlooms for generations yet to be born!

The
Patterns

Pieced and hand-quilted by the author, using reproduction fabrics.

Whimsy

T his newly-created quilt is a combination of two interesting blocks: the pinwheel center and the outer "star" sashing which comes from a block named *Ish River Rose*. I loved the circular shape and motion of the pinwheel block, and thought the outer star frame would be the perfect setting for the pinwheel center, with smaller pinwheels making up the cornerstones. Quilts with secondary designs are always intriguing, and are interesting to piece!

Quilt shown, 64" x 76", 20 blocks, 4 x 5 setting
Larger size: 88" x 100", 42 blocks, 6 x 7 setting

Tool Requirements

Tri-Recs™
Tri-Mate™ (optional; using this tool will eliminate the seam in the center of the horizontal star point unit.)
Easy Angle™
Companion Angle™

Fabric Requirements

White: 2¾ yd. (4¾ yd.)
Prints: Variety of prints totaling 2 yd. (4 yd.)
Blue solid: 3 yd. (4¼ yd.); includes binding
Backing: 3¾ yd. (7¾ yd.)

Note: If you prefer to cut your border strips lengthwise, skip down to that section and cut the borders first. Cut the remaining pieces from the leftovers.

Cutting Directions for Large Pinwheel Blocks

From	Cut	To Yield
White	7(13) – 2½" strips	80(168) Companion Angle triangles
	10(21) – 1½" strips	80(168) 1½" x 5" rectangles
Variety of prints	3½" strips	80(168) Easy Angle triangles
	2½" strips	80(168) Companion Angle triangles

Note: If not using Companion Angle, cut 20(42) – 5¼" squares, cut twice on the diagonal. If not using Easy Angle, cut 40(84) – 3⅞" squares. Cut once on the diagonal for triangles.

Large Pinwheel Block Assembly

Layer the 80(168) white and print Companion Angle triangles right sides together. Sew on the right edge of the triangles with the *print* triangle on top. Press toward the print triangle.

Sew the 80 (168) white rectangles to the base of the Easy Angle print triangles. Layer the print triangle right sides together with the white rectangle. Sew with the triangle on top. Press toward the triangle. Using the Easy Angle, trim the triangle to the 4½" size.

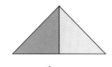

Join the two different kinds of triangles as shown to make a square. Repeat for the remaining triangles. Press the seams as shown. Make 80(168) squares. At this point, the square should measure 4½".

Join the squares in pairs, pressing as indicated. Join the two rows and press the seam open. At this point, the block should measure 8½".

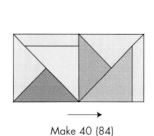

Make 40 (84)

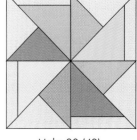

Make 20 (42)

Cutting Directions for Star Points

From	Cut	To Yield
White	13(25) – 2½" strips	98(194) Tri-Mate triangles*
Blue solid	7(13) – 4½" strips	98(194) Tri triangles

*If not using Tri-Mate, cut 9(17) – 4½" white strips. Cut 98(194) *pairs* of Recs triangles. Make 98(194) Tri-Recs units (see page 124). Join the units point to point. Press the center seam open.

Note: There are no substitutes for the Tri-Recs or Tri-Mate tools.

Star Point Assembly

Sew a blue Tri triangle to the right side of a white Tri-Mate triangle. Use the cut-off point on the Tri-Mate to help align the blue Tri triangle. Press toward the blue Tri triangle. Repeat to make 98(194) units.

Join the units created above, matching the cut-off points at each end of the units and the centers. Press the seam either direction. At this point, the unit should measure 4½" x 8½". Make 49(97) of these star point units.

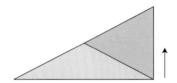

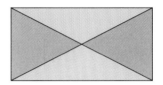

Cutting Directions for Small Pinwheels

From	Cut	To Yield
White	5(9) – 2½" strips	120(224) Easy Angle triangles*
Variety of prints	2½" strips	120(224) Easy Angle triangles*

*Layer the print and white strips right sides together, and cut with the Easy Angle. They will then be ready to chain sew.

Note: If not using Easy Angle, cut 60(112) – 2⅞" squares of both fabrics. Cut once on the diagonal.

Small Pinwheel Block Assembly

Join all the triangles to make triangle squares. Press toward the print fabric. Join the triangle squares in pairs. Make 60(112) pairs. Press as indicated.

point the pinwheel block should measure 4½".

Join the sets of triangle squares to make 30(56) small pinwheel blocks. Press the seam open. At this

Quilt Assembly

When all the units have been sewn and pressed, you can start to assemble the quilt. Assemble 5 (7) small pinwheel blocks and 4 (6) star point units in 6 (8) rows like this:

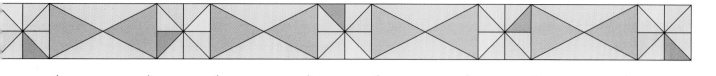

Assemble 5 (7) rows with 4 (6) large pinwheel blocks and 5 (7) vertical star point units like this: Press as indicated by the arrows.

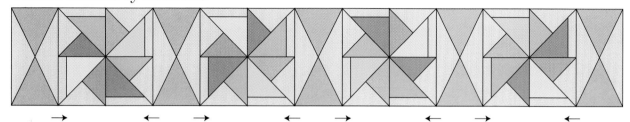

Join the rows, matching and pinning at the seam intersections. Press the rows toward the large pinwheel blocks.

Cutting Directions for Borders

From	Cut	To Yield
Blue solid	7 (9) – 3" strips	First border
	7 (10) – 2½" strips	Last border
	2¼" bias strips	Binding
White	5 (7) – 2½" strips	4 squares
		124 (172) Easy Angle triangles*
Variety of prints	2½" strips	124 (172) Easy Angle triangles*

*Layer the print and white strips right sides together and cut with Easy Angle. They will then be ready to chain sew.

Note: If not using Easy Angle, cut 62 (86) – 2⅞" squares. Cut once on the diagonal.

Adding the Borders

The first blue border acts like a spacer border. The mathematically perfect measurement for this border should be 2½". However, most people (myself included) do not sew perfectly, and a little extra "fudge" room is built into this first border.

Join the border strips with diagonal seams pressed open. Sew the first blue border to the quilt top. (See page 19 for instruction on adding borders.)
Piece all the triangle squares. Press toward the print. For each of the top and bottom saw-toothed borders, join 28 (40) triangle squares, 14 (20) facing one direc-

tion, 14(20) the other. Press the seams toward the prints, except for the center, which is pressed open.In the same manner, piece the side borders with 34(46) in each border, 17(23) facing one direction, 17(23) the other. Press in the same manner.

Centering the pieced top and bottom border, check to see if the sides of the first border need to be trimmed. The pieced border should equal the *width of the quilt top*. If the quilt top is wider than the pieced border, trim the sides *evenly* to fit. (See page 20 for instruction on adding pieced borders.)

Before sewing on the top and bottom borders, check if the length of the pieced side borders matches the length of the quilt sides. Trim *evenly* as needed.

Sew the pieced borders to the top and bottom of the quilt. Press toward the blue border. Add the white squares to both ends of the side-pieced borders. Press toward the white square. Sew the pieced borders to the sides of the quilt. Press toward the blue border.

Piece, measure, trim, and sew the last blue solid borders to the quilt. (See page 19 for instruction on adding borders.)

Finishing the Quilt

Mark the quilt top, baste, and quilt. The quilt shown was partially quilted by hand and partially by machine. It was machine stitched in the ditch through the diagonals of the pinwheel blocks and the small pinwheels. Hand quilting accents were added in the large pinwheels. The white and blue triangles in the star points were hand-stitched ¼" from the seam lines. The first border was quilted with a small cable design. The pieced and outer borders were quilted in diagonal lines following the seam lines of the triangles.

Binding

Before binding, hand or machine baste (with a walking foot) a scant ¼" from the edge of the quilt. This is to keep the layers from shifting while the binding is being sewn on. Prepare and sew the binding to the quilt with a ¼" seam. Trim off excess batting and backing, then turn the binding to the backside of the quilt and stitch down by hand with matching thread. (See page 21 for instruction on binding.)

Sign and date your heirloom creation!

Whimsy

Reproduction fabrics, pieced and machine quilted by author.

Hugs and Kisses

See the X's and O's formed by the design? We could call this the Tic Tac Toe quilt, but doesn't it also remind you of the X's and O's after your signature on a letter to a loved one? Piece the quilt as shown in the fresh colors of blue and yellow, or choose a different color background and make the triangles from a variety of colors.

Quilt shown: 60" x 84", 24 — 12" blocks, 4 x 6 setting
Larger size: 84" x 96", 42 blocks, 6 x 7 setting

Tool Requirement

Easy Angle

Fabric Requirements

Yellow background: 5⅓ yd. (7½ yd.)
Blue prints: ¼ yd. of 10 (16) different prints; ½ yd. (⅔ yd.) of one print for larger triangles
Backing: 5 yd. (7½ yd.)

Note: You may choose to cut your borders first from the length of the fabric to avoid piecing them later. If so, cut 4 yellow inner borders 3½" wide and 4 yellow outer borders 2½" wide. Cut the approximate length you will need and add an extra 4" for insurance. Set aside.

Cutting Directions

From	Cut	To Yield
Yellow	7(13) – 4½" strips	48(84) 4½" squares
		24(42) Easy Angle triangles*
	28(46) – 2½" strips	704(1,172) Easy Angle triangles*
		4 — 2½" squares (for corners of pieced border)
	7(9) – 3½" strips	First border
	9(10) – 2½" strips	Third border
	2¼" bias strips	Binding
One blue print	2(3) – 4½" strips	24(42) Easy Angle triangles*
Variety of blue prints	28(46) – 2½" strips	704(1,172) Easy Angle triangles*

*Layer blue and yellow strips, right sides together, and cut Easy Angle triangles. They will then be ready for chain piecing.

Note: If not using Easy Angle, cut squares 4⅞" and 2⅞" respectively, cut once on the diagonal.

Block Assembly

Assemble all the small (2½") and large (4½") triangle squares. Press toward the print fabrics. Trim dog-ears.

Sew 576(1,008) of the small triangle squares together into sets of four. (The remaining triangle squares will be used in the saw-tooth border.) Press the seams as shown. At this point the units should measure 4½" square. Make 144(252) units.

Join the pieced triangle units, the plain squares, and the large pieced triangle square into 3 rows as shown. Press as indicated.

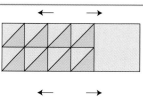

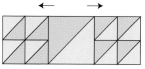

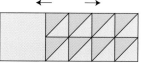

Join the rows to make a block. At this point the block should measure 12½" square. Make 24(42) blocks.

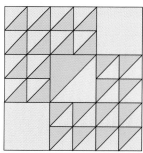

Quilt Assembly

Arrange the blocks as shown, or devise your own setting. When the blocks have been arranged to your satisfaction, join the blocks in rows. Press the joining seams in each row in alternate directions. Join the rows. Press.

Borders

First border (see page 19 for instruction on adding borders): Measure the width of the quilt in several places. Take an average of this measurement if needed. Using the 3½" wide yellow borders, trim two borders this length. Sew to the top and bottom of the quilt. Press toward the borders.

Repeat this procedure for the sides of the quilt.

Second border: Join 26(38) triangle squares for the top border, with the triangles pointing out from the center. Repeat for the bottom border. Trim the quilt top *evenly* to fit the pieced borders. *Do not sew these borders to the quilt until you have pieced, measured, and trimmed the quilt to fit the side borders!* See page 20 for instruction on adding pieced borders.

Join 38(44) triangle squares for one side of the quilt, pointing out from the center. Repeat for the second side border. Trim the quilt top evenly to fit the pieced borders.

Sew the top and bottom borders to the quilt. Press toward the plain border.

Sew the yellow corner squares to the ends of the side-pieced borders. Sew to the sides of the quilt. Press toward the plain borders.

Third border: Add the last plain border to the quilt following the directions for adding borders on page 19.

Finishing the Quilt

Mark any quilting designs, then layer and baste. A floral design was machine quilted in the open squares formed by the intersections of the blocks. Half and quarter designs were quilted along the edges and corners. A small machine meander was quilted around the design, and in all the yellow background areas using matching thread. The blue triangles are not quilted.

Binding

Before binding, hand or machine baste (using a walking foot) a scant ¼" from the edge of the quilt to keep the layers from shifting while the binding is sewn on. The quilt was bound in double bias binding in yellow, cut at 2¼".

Don't forget to sign and date the quilt with hugs and kisses!

Tip:

Alternate cutting, sewing, and pressing of triangles. It reduces fatique and tedium.

Hugs and Kisses

Designed, pieced and hand-quilted by Lanie Tiffenbach.

Scrap Baskets

Basket quilts have been popular for a long, long time. Before plastic or paper bags were used for packaging (which didn't happen until the '50s) women used baskets for grocery shopping, gathering eggs or garden vegetables, and as "scrap baskets" for quiltmaking. The scrappy baskets are joined with a Garden Maze sashing, and the quilt is made extra-special with the use of an ice-cream cone border.

Tool Requirement
Easy Angle

Fabric Requirements
White: 6¾ yd.
Gold: 3 yd.
Prints: fat eighths, fat quarters or ¼ yd. of 25 different prints
Backing: 7½ yd.

Cutting Directions for Basket Blocks

From	Cut	To Yield
White	4 – 4½" strips	50 Easy Angle triangles
	12 – 2½" strips	100 rectangles 2½" x 4½"
	10 – 2½" strips	250 Easy Angle triangles
From each print cut	1 – 4½" strip	4 Easy Angle triangles
	1 – 2½" strip	14 Easy Angle triangles

Note: If not using Easy Angle, cut 4⅞" and 2⅞" squares respectively; cut once on the diagonal.

Basket Block Assembly
(Make 50 blocks)
For each block you will need:
5 small triangle squares of the same print and white
2 different large print triangles
2 small triangles, the same print as one of the large triangles
2 – 2½" x 4½" white rectangles
1 large white triangle

HINT: Place all the pieces for one block on individual paper plates. They can be stacked and ready by your sewing machine when you have a few minutes to sew.

Assemble five small (2½") triangle squares of white and the same print. Press toward the print triangles.

Join two different 4½" Easy Angle print triangles to make a large triangle square. Press either direction.

Join the small triangle squares into one set of two squares, and one set of three squares as shown. Press.

Sew the smaller triangle unit to the left side of the large triangle square. Press toward the large square.

Sew the larger triangle unit to the top of the previous unit. Press toward the large square.

Choose two small print triangles to match the print at the bottom of the basket. Sew the small triangles to the ends of the white rectangles, one for the right side of the basket, one for the left. Press the seams toward the print triangle.

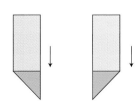

Sew to the sides of the baskets. Press as shown.

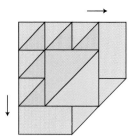

Sew the large white triangle to the base of the basket. Press toward the white triangle. At this point, the basket blocks should measure 8½". Make 50 blocks.

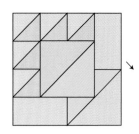

Cutting Directions for Sashing, Side & Corner Triangles, Borders

From	Cut	To Yield
White	65 – 1¼" strips	Strip sets
	3 – 17" strips	5 – 17" squares cut twice on the diagonal for 18 side triangles (2 will be left over)
		2 – 10" squares, cut once on the diagonal for corner triangles
	7 – 4¼" strips	140 "A" wedges for ice cream cone border*
Gold	40 – 1¼" strips	Strip sets
	10 – 1¼" strips	Border
	1¼" *bias* strips	Binding
Variety of Prints (from each print cut:)		6 or 7 "B" wdges for ice cream cone border*

*A and B templates for wedges can be found on page 41.

Note: The side and corner triangles are slightly larger than needed, and will be trimmed later.

Sashing

Make 30 strip sets of white-gold-white. Press the seams toward the gold strip, making sure to press the strip sets straight, not curved. Cut into 120 – 2¾" x 8½" (or the size of your blocks) sashes. Use the remainder of the strip sets in the next step.

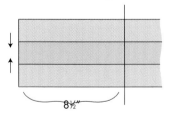

8½"

HINT: To keep the strip sets from curving, finger press the seams before ironing. When ironing, lay the strip sets the short way on the ironing board.

Cornerstone Blocks

To make the cornerstone blocks, cut 71 – 1¼" wide units from the remainder of the sashing strip sets. Set aside.

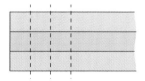

From the remaining white and gold strips, sew together 5 strip sets of gold-white-gold. Press toward the gold strips. Cut apart into 142 – 1¼" units.

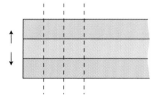

Assemble 71 nine-patch cornerstone units from the two different pieced units. Press toward the outside of the block. The nine-patch units should measure 2¾" square unfinished.

Quilt Assembly

Lay out the quilt in diagonal rows, with sashing and cornerstones between the blocks, and side and corner triangles along the outside edges of the quilt top. Sew the units together in diagonal rows, pressing the seams toward the sashing. Sew the diagonal rows together, pressing toward the sashing. Add the corner triangles last.

Carefully trim the quilt edges, keeping the corners square, and *leaving ¼" seam allowance at the corners of the nine-patch corner blocks*.

Borders

Piece 1¼" gold strips as necessary for the inside borders with diagonal seams pressed open. Measure, trim, and sew the borders to the quilt top. (See page 19 for instruction on adding borders.)

For the top and bottom borders, sew together 33 print wedges with 32 white wedges, beginning and ending with a print wedge. Add one more print wedge to both ends of the borders. The *bottom* raw edge of the pieced border should match the raw edge of the top and bottom of the quilt. Note the wide edge of the wedge extends beyond the edge of the quilt. If the pieced border does not fit properly, you can make slight adjustments to the seams between the wedges or trim the gold border slightly.

The side borders are pieced of 39 print wedges and 38 white wedges, beginning and ending with a print wedge. Add one more print wedge to both ends of the borders. Again, adjust as necessary. Sew the borders to the quilt top. Join the 4 print wedges at the corners.

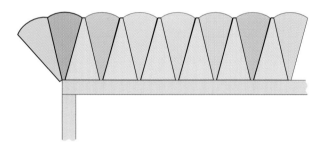

Finishing the Quilt

Mark any quilting designs on the quilt top. Layer, baste, and quilt. The quilt shown was hand-quilted ¼" from the seams around the basket, and inside both large print triangles that make up the basket. The sashing and cornerstones were stitched in the ditch on both sides of the white strips. A pretty design was quilted in each of the large outside triangles. A line of quilting was done in the ditch on both sides of the gold border. The wedges in the border were quilted in the ditch between each wedge.

Binding

Before binding, hand or machine baste (using a walking foot) a scant ¼" from the edge of the quilt. This will prevent the layers from shifting while the binding is being sewn on.

From one yard of gold, cut *bias* binding strips at 1¼" wide. Join with diagonal seams pressed open. You will need approximately 450". Sew to the quilt with a ¼" seam allowance, pivoting at the inside corners. (See page 128 for instruction on binding a scalloped edge.)

Sign and date your delectable quilt!

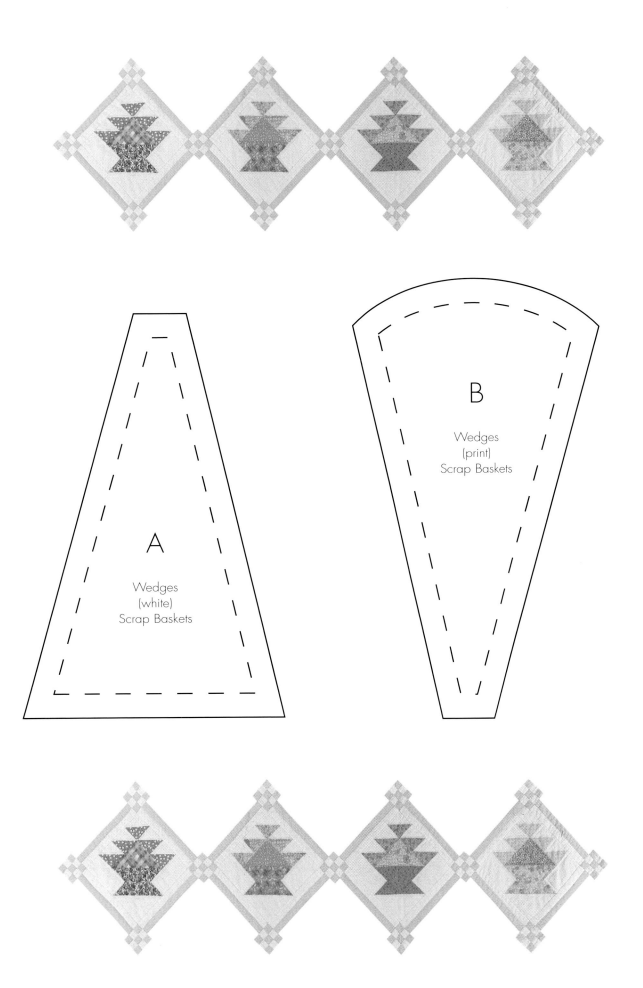

A

Wedges
(white)
Scrap Baskets

B

Wedges
(print)
Scrap Baskets

Reproduction fabrics, pieced and machine quilted by author.

ℬaby 𝒫uzzle

ave you been collecting those darling reproduction novelty prints and wondered how to use them in a project? This variation of the Log Cabin block is a very easy project, making the piecing a snap! Just as with a Log Cabin block, you can arrange the blocks in various ways for different effects. Create your own puzzle quilt!

Fabric Requirements (quilt shown was made in flannel)

15 different prints: ¼ yd. (or fat quarters) of each
Red print for block center: ⅛ yd.
Binding: ⅜ yd.
Backing: 1⅜ yd.

Cutting Directions

From	Cut	To Yield
Red	2- 2" strips	30 – 2" squares
Each fabric strips, cut a total of:	Cut five 1¼" x 40" strips (or, nine 1¼" x 20" strips) from *each* fabric. Using these	

4 – 1¼" x 2" rectangles
8 – 1¼" x 3½" rectangles
8 – 1¼" x 5" rectangles
8 – 1¼" x 6½" rectangles
4 – 1¼" x 8" rectangles

Block Assembly

The A and B sides of the block use the 2", 3½", 5", and 6½" rectangles. The C and D sides of the block use 3½", 5", 6½", and 8" rectangles.

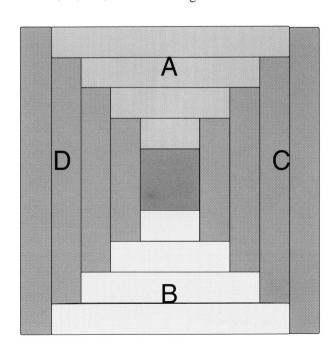

Using two different fabrics, sew 1¼" x 2" A and B rectangles to opposite sides of the red square. Press toward the rectangles.

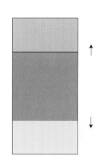

Using two different fabrics, sew 1¼" x 3½" C and D rectangles to opposite sides of the pieced unit. Press toward the strips just added.

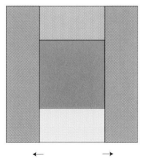

Sew 1¼" x 3½" A and B rectangles to opposite sides of the pieced units, matching prints. Press toward the strips just added.

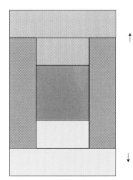

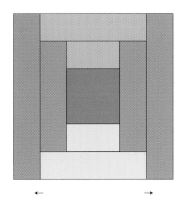

Add the 1¼" x 5" C and D rectangles to the long sides of the unit. Press toward the strips just added.

Continue adding rectangles in this manner to the block, alternating A and B rectangles, then C and D rectangles until the block measures 8" unfinished. Make a total of 30 blocks.

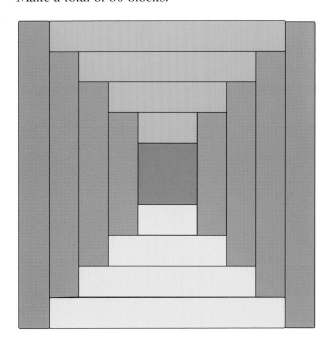

Quilt Assembly

Sew the blocks together in rows of 5, alternating long (unseamed) and short sides. Press the seams toward the long sides. Make 6 rows.

Note: Experiment with different layouts of the blocks before sewing.

Sew the rows together, matching seam intersections. Press the rows all one direction.

Finishing the Quilt

Mark any quilting designs. Layer, baste, and quilt. The quilt shown was machine-stitched in the ditch on the diagonal following the "stair steps" created by the design.

Before basting, hand or machine baste (with a walking foot) a scant ¼" from the edge of the quilt. This prevents the layers from shifting while the binding is being sewn on.

Bind with double-fold straight-of-grain binding cut at 2¼". (See page 21 for instruction on binding.)

Sign and date your quilted keepsake for that new baby!

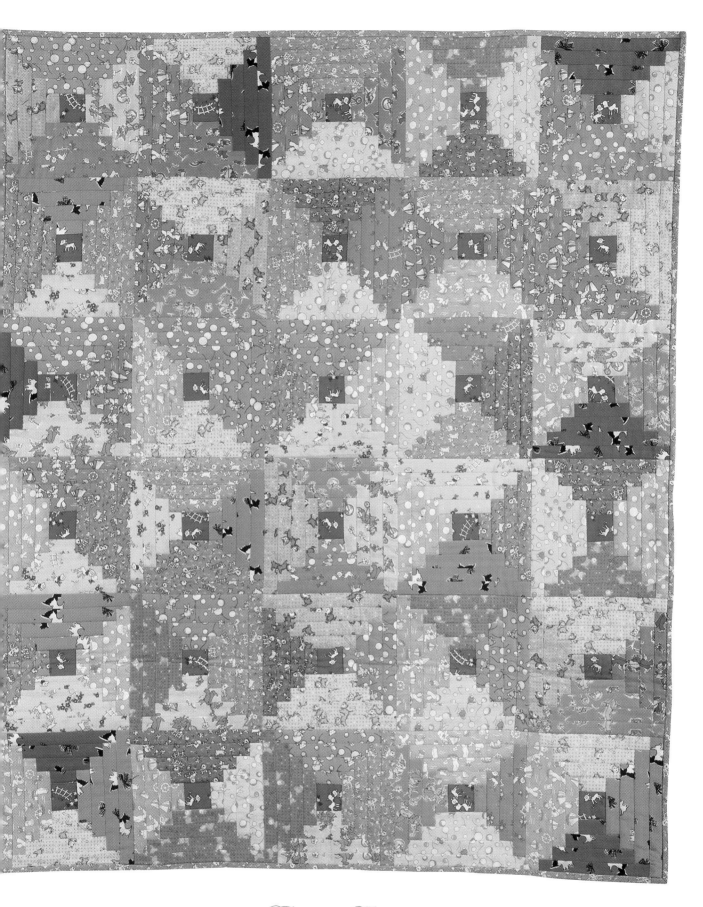

Baby Puzzle

Pieced and hand and machine-quilted by the author with reproduction fabrics.

Grandma's Strippy Quilt

Strippy quilts (quilts pieced in long rows instead of the typical block construction) have a long history. Very old English quilts frequently employ this method of construction.

Following this old tradition, I made a strippy quilt with a yellow background, and when I was hand-quilting on it over Easter, my sisters- and mother-in-law were quite taken with it. It reminded them of a quilt given to them by their Grandma Becker, which unfortunately had not survived the years. An old picture was found of her and her neighbor lady quilting on "the" yellow strippy quilt. What a coincidence that I should make a similar quilt many years later!

Quilt shown: 69" x 77"
Larger size: 85" x 90"

Tool Requirements

Companion Angle
Easy Angle

Fabric Requirements

Yellow solid: 3¾ yd.(4½ yd.)
Assorted prints: 14(21) ⅓ yds; 5 yd. total (7¼ yd. total)
Backing: 4¼ yd.(7½ yd.)

Cutting Directions

From	Cut	To Yield
Yellow solid	80"(90") lengthwise	5(6) 4" strips for vertical sashes and side borders
		2 – 4" strips for top and bottom borders
	12(18) 2" strips	200(290) Companion Angle triangles
	1 – 2¼" strip	16(20) Easy Angle triangles
From each print	3 – 2½" strips	Cut 12 – 2½" x 10½" rectangles

Note: If not using Companion Angle, cut 50(73) 4¼" squares, cut twice on the diagonal. If not using Easy Angle, cut 8(10) 2⅝" squares, cut once on the diagonal.

Piecing the Strips

Randomly sew 20(30) sets of 4 – 2½" x 10½" assorted print rectangles together lengthwise, and 20(30) sets of three 2½" x 10½" print rectangles together lengthwise. (The remainder of the strips will be used later.) Press the seams all one direction. (With your fingernail, crease the seams to one side, then iron.) Cut all the sets into 2½" segments.

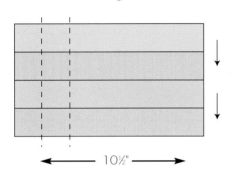

← 10½" →

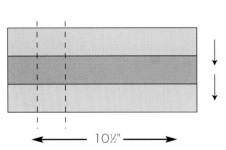

← 10½" →

Join a strip of four squares to a strip of three squares to make a seven-square unit. Make 80(120) units. (With this method of constructing the seven-square units, you can achieve better diversity.) You will need 20(24) seven-square units for each of the 4(5) vertical pieced strips on the quilt.

Sew a Companion Angle triangle to both ends of these units. Sew all the Companion Angles on as shown. This will guarantee the triangles are sewn on correctly. Press the seams all one direction.

Sew 20(24) seven-square units together as shown, turning the units as needed to alternate the seams. Press the seams all one direction. Make 4(5) pieced strips.

Cut the remainder of the 2½" strips into squares. Piece together the corner units as shown below. Use the yellow Easy Angle triangles at the top corners. (You will need to replace a Companion Angle with an Easy Angle to complete other the corners correctly.) You will need 8(10) corner units. Join the corner units to both ends of the 4(5) pieced strips.

Press the seams all one direction. Trim the pieced strips evenly, *leaving a ¼" seam allowance from the corners of the squares*. The yellow edge triangles are slightly larger than needed to allow for trimming.

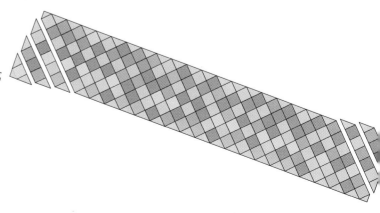

Assembling the Quilt

Measure the length of the strippy units through the center. Take an average of these measurements if necessary. Trim 5(6) of the 4" sashes/borders to this length. Sew the sashes between the strippy units.

TIP: Sew with the yellow sash on top; this will prevent the pieced strips from stretching.

Sew the remaining two sashes/borders to the sides of the quilt.

Take a measurement of the width of the quilt in several places. Trim the remaining two border pieces to this length. Sew to the top and bottom of the quilt.

Cutting Directions for Pieced Border

From	Cut	To Yield
Yellow solid	11(13) 2" strips	180(208) Companion Angle triangles
	2 – 2¼" strips	32 Easy Angle triangles
Variety of prints		98(112) 2½" squares

Note: The yellow triangles are slightly larger than needed to allow for trimming.

Note: If not using Companion Angle, cut 45(52) 4¼" squares, cut twice on the diagonal. If not using Easy Angle, cut 16 – 2⅝" squares, cut once on the diagonal.

Assembling the Pieced Border

You will need 22(25) print squares each for the top and bottom borders. Sew Companion Angle triangles to both sides of 20(23) squares as shown. Press toward the print square. Join the units to make a long border strip.

Make two end pieces as shown, using Easy Angle triangles on the ends. Sew to both ends of the pieced border. Press all the seams one direction. Make 2.

The top- and bottom-pieced borders need to be the same measurement as the width of the quilt. Trim the sides of the quilt *evenly* to equal the length of the top and bottom borders. Set aside.

Make two side borders in the same manner with a total of 25(29) squares for each border. Use the Easy Angle triangles on both ends as before.

Before sewing on the top and bottom borders, measure the *length* of the quilt. The measurement of the length of the quilt should equal the length of the pieced side borders. If not, trim the *top and bottom* yellow borders evenly. *The quilt measurements should now equal the measurements of the borders.* Now you may sew the pieced borders to the top and bottom of the quilt, stitching with the yellow border on top to prevent stretching the pieced border. Press the seam toward the yellow border.

With the remaining 2½" print squares, sew yellow Easy Angle triangles to all four sides of the print squares to make four square-within-a-square units for the corners.

Make 4

Sew the corner units to both ends of the side borders. Press toward the corner unit. Sew the pieced side borders to the quilt, sewing with the yellow border on top. Press the seams toward the yellow border.

Finishing the Quilt

Mark any quilting designs on the quilt top. Cut batting and backing 4" larger than the quilt top. Baste the three layers together and quilt as desired. The quilt shown was machine quilted in a meander over the pieced strips. A flower/vine was hand quilted in the yellow sashes and borders. The border squares were quilted ¼" from the seam allowance on both sides.

Binding

Before binding, baste a scant ¼" from the edge of the quilt to keep the layers from shifting while the binding is being sewn on.

Cut four 2¼" lengths of binding from the remainder of the 80"(90") long yellow solid fabric strip from which the borders were cut. Join the binding strips with diagonal seams pressed open. Fold the binding in half, wrong sides together and press. Sew the binding to the right side of the quilt with a ¼" seam allowance. Turn to the back and hand sew in place with matching thread. (See page 21 for instructions on binding.)

Sign and date your masterpiece!

Reproduction fabrics. Basket design by Rachel Shelburne, pieced, hand-appliqued and hand-quilted by author.

Peek-A-Boo Baskets

This lovely basket reminds one of fancy curved baskets for flowers and also the elaborate Easter bonnets of a time past. This newly designed basket has a charming posy peeking out. The baskets are all cut from reproduction '30s solids just as in the old kit quilts. The latticework of scraps is simply a Puss-in-the-Corner block that alternates with the basket block. Simple to piece and appliqué, you will enjoy making this basket quilt and it will reward you with the delights of springtime in your home.

Tool Requirements

Large Square
Easy Scallop (optional)

Fabric Requirements

White: 3¾ yd.(6¼ yd.)
Variety of prints: 7¼ yd. or fat quarters, 1¾ yd. total (9¼ yd. or 2¼ yd. total)
Green solid: 3¾ yd.(4½ yd.)
Solids: ¼ yd (½ yd.) of 5 or more solids
Backing: 5¼ yd.(8 yd.)

Optional Supplies

Freezer paper
Lightweight cardboard
Fusible webbing

Cutting Directions

From	Cut	To Yield
White	6(11) – 11" strips	17(31) – 11" squares for basket blocks
	5(8) – 2½" strips	19(32) – 2½" x 10½" rectangles for Strip Set A and B
	6(8) – 6½" strips	9(16) – 6½" x 10½" rectangles for Strip Set C
		36(64) – 2½" x 6½" rectangles
	5 (6) – 2½" strips	66(86) – 2½" squares
Variety of prints		41(72) – 2½" x 10½" rectangles
		66(86) – 2½" squares

Directions for Puss-in-the-Corner Blocks

Make 18(32) blocks.
Sew two different print 2½" x 10½" rectangles on either side of a white 2½" x 10½" rectangle. Press the seams toward the prints. This is Strip Set A. Make 9(16) different strip sets. Cut into 36(64) – 2½" wide units.

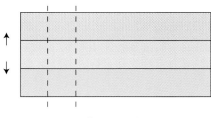

Strip set A

Sew together two white 2½" x 10½" rectangles and one print rectangle. Press the seams toward the print. This is Strip Set B. Make 5(8) different strip sets. Cut into 18(32) – 2½" wide units.

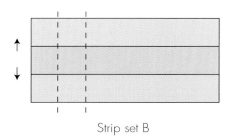

Strip set B

Sew together two different Strip Set A units and one of Strip Set B. Press toward the center strip. Make 18(32) nine-patch units.

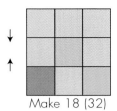

Make 18 (32)

Sew two different print 2½" x 10½" rectangles on both long sides of the 6½" x 10½" white rectangles. Press toward the white rectangles. This is Strip Set C. Make 9(16) strip sets. Cut into 36(64) – 2½" wide units.

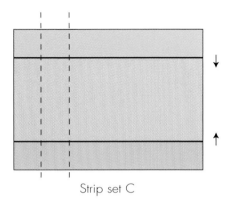

Strip set C

Sew 2½" x 6½" white rectangles to the top and bottom of the nine-patch blocks. Press toward the white rectangles. Make 18(32) of these units.

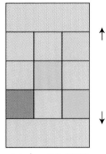

Make 18 (32)

Sew two different Strip Set C's to the sides of the nine-patch blocks. Press toward the units just added. Make 18(32) of these *Puss-in-the-Corner* blocks. They should measure 10½" square at this point.

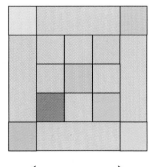

← Make 18 (32) →

Directions for Basket Blocks
Make 17(31) basket blocks.

Note: You can use any method of appliqué you choose. See pages 18-19 for more appliqué options.

Before cutting any appliqué shapes, measure and cut off 90" (115") of the green solid. Set aside for the outside borders. The remainder of the fabric is used for baskets and bias binding.

Trace the two pieces of the basket (templates given on page 57) onto the dull side of the freezer paper. Note the design is reversed, but will appear correctly on the quilt block.

TIP: You can use the same freezer paper template a number of times.

Cut out the two shapes on the marked line. With a warm iron, press the two templates to the wrong side of the solid fabric you have chosen for the basket. Cut out the shapes, adding a scant ¼" seam allowance. Clip any inside curves and corners. Press the seam allowances over the edge of the freezer paper with the warm iron or with your fingers. Remove the freezer paper. (See page 18-19 for instruction on appliqué and more options.)

Fold the background square into quarters and lightly crease to mark the center lines of the block to help you center the basket. The basket is placed straight on the square (not on point). Baste or pin the basket shape in place. Appliqué, using matching thread. Note the flower is tucked inside the basket and needs to be appliquéd in place before the basket appliqué is finished.

Note: The background square is slightly larger than needed, and will be trimmed later.

Following the same procedure, appliqué the leaves in place on the block. If the basket shadows through the flower, trim away underneath the flower.

For making perfect circles for the flower center, cut a circle template out of lightweight cardboard. Trace around the circle on the wrong side of the fabric chosen for the flower center. Cut out, adding a scant ¼" seam allowance. Run a line of basting around the circle outside of the marked line. Place the template in the center, and pull the basting stitches tight to gather the edges over the template. Press, and then remove the template. Appliqué in place.

Appliqué 17(31) basket blocks. Press, then trim the finished blocks evenly to 10½" square.

Quilt Assembly
Lay out the quilt blocks in rows, beginning with a *Puss-in-the-Corner* block and alternating with appliquéd basket blocks. Press the seams toward the basket blocks.

Sew the rows together, pressing the seams all one direction. At this point the quilt center should measure 50½" x 70½" (70½" x 90½").

Borders

From the 90"(115") length of green solid, trim off the selvages, and then cut *lengthwise* four 5"(6") wide outer borders and four 2½" inner borders.

Measure and trim two 2½" wide inner borders the width of the quilt. Sew to the top and bottom of the quilt. (See page 19 for instructions on adding borders.) Press toward the green borders.

Measure and trim two 2½" wide inner borders the length of the quilt, including the borders just added. Sew to the sides of the quilt. Press toward the borders.

Pieced Border

For the top and bottom borders, alternating white and print squares, sew together a total of 27(37) squares, beginning and ending with a print square. Press the seams toward the print squares.

Sew the pieced borders to the top and bottom of the quilt, lining up the seams with the seams in the pieced blocks.

Note: If the pieced border does not fit properly, you can adjust the seams in the pieced border to make it fit, or trim the green border evenly.

Press toward the green border.

For the side borders, alternating white and print squares, sew together a total of 39(49) squares, beginning and ending with a white square. Press the seams toward the print squares.

Sew the pieced borders to the sides of the quilt, lining up the seams with the seams in the pieced blocks. (Again, you can adjust the seams in the pieced border if needed.) Press toward the green borders.

Outer Border

Measure and trim two 5"(6") borders the width of the quilt. (See page 19 for instruction on adding borders.) Sew to the top and bottom of the quilt. Press the seams toward the green border.

Measure and trim two 5"(6") borders the length of the quilt. Sew to the sides of the quilt. Press the seams toward the green border.

Finishing the Quilt

Mark any quilting designs before layering the quilt. The scallop edge can be marked at this point or after the quilting is completed. (See page 127 for instructions on marking a scalloped edge.) Prepare a backing and batting that is at least 4" larger than the quilt top. Baste the three layers together.

The quilt shown was quilted in a diagonal grid behind the baskets. The baskets, leaves, and flowers were outline-quilted. The squares in the *Puss-in-the-Corner* blocks were quilted ¼" from the seams inside the squares.

The first border was quilted with a leaf design, and the pieced and solid outer border were quilted with straight lines 1" apart.

Binding

If you haven't already done so, mark the scalloped edge on the quilt top. Baste by hand (or with a walking foot on the machine) on the marked line. This will prevent the layers from shifting while the binding is being sewn on. ***Do not cut on this line!***

Cut 1¼" bias strips of green solid for binding. (See page 21 for instruction on cutting bias binding.) Join with diagonal seams pressed open. Sew to the quilt top with a ¼" seam, using the marked line as the "edge" of your quilt to align the binding. The edges are trimmed to ¼" seam allowance after the binding has been sewn on. (See page 128 for instructions on binding a curved edge.) Turn the binding to the back side and stitch down by hand.

Don't forget to add a label to your heirloom quilt!

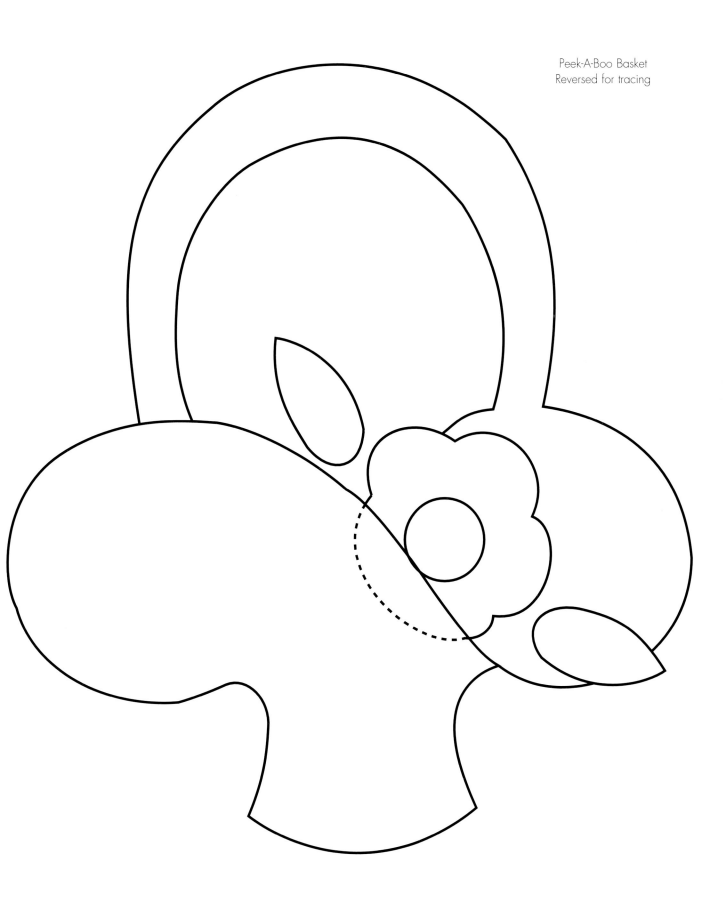

Vintage blocks made mid-30s by Grace Belle Weatherwax, recently finished and hand-quilted by Jeri Hillmeier.

Butterfly

Friendship Quilt

Butterfly quilts first appeared in the 1920s, and were symbols of hope in the dark days of war and the Great Depression. Butterflies were a hopeful reminder that better times would come again someday. This particular butterfly quilt was also a Friendship quilt – a quilt style that has been popular for more than a century and continues to be popular today.

A Friendship quilt is one presented to someone by a group of friends, or is a collection of blocks made by friends. For this Butterfly Friendship quilt, friends of Grace each gave her a fabric square to make a butterfly. Grace then appliquéd the butterfly blocks and, on a slip of paper, pinned their names to each block, and set the blocks together with the yellow sashing. The quilt top was packed away, forgotten until discovered by a great-niece years later. This niece, Jeri Hillmeier, added the narrow blue border of reproduction fabric and the wider outside border of muslin and hand-quilted the precious heirloom. She wrote each of the names of her aunt's friends in the lower right-hand corner of each block.

You can re-create this Friendship Butterfly quilt by asking your friends to sew a block for you, or a group of friends could surprise someone dear with a set of blocks or finished quilt. See Design Options at the end for more ways to set your Butterfly blocks.

Tool Requirement

Large Square

Fabric Requirements

White: 7 yd.
Yellow solid: 1⅔ yd.
Blue print: 1¾ yd.
Assorted prints: 10" square for each of 30 butterflies
Backing: 7⅞ yd.

Optional Supplies

Freezer paper
Black embroidery floss or #8 pearl cotton

Cutting Directions

From	Cut	To Yield
White	40" x 106"	4 – 8" x 106" outer borders
	10 – 13" strips	30 – 13" squares
Yellow solid	2 – 12½" strips	24 – 2¾" x 12½" sashes
	10 – 2¾" strips	5 – 2¾" x 72" horizontal sashes, pieced
		4 – 2¾" cornerstone squares
Blue print	8 – 2¾" strips	Inner border
	2¼" bias strips	Bias binding

Butterfly Blocks

Cut an assortment of butterflies from the print fabrics. Use the template given on page 62. (See pages 18-19 for more appliqué options.) Note the butterfly is cut in one piece with the lines added in embroidery. Trace the butterfly shape onto the dull side of freezer paper. Cut out the butterfly shape carefully on the marked line. With a warm iron, press the freezer paper shape to the wrong side of the print fabric. Cut out, adding a scant ¼" seam allowance. Clip any inside curves. Press the seam allowance over the freezer paper with the iron. Remove the freezer paper.

Crease the background square lightly into quarters. Use the creases to center the butterfly on the block.

Note: The butterfly is set straight on the block, but you may choose to set the butterfly on point.

By hand, baste the butterfly to the background square close to the edge of the butterfly. By hand or machine, buttonhole-stitch the butterflies to the background. At this point you may choose to cut away the background fabric behind the butterfly. Add the embroidery details. Complete all the butterfly blocks in this same manner. Make 30 blocks. **Trim the blocks to 12½".**

Quilt Assembly

Sew the butterfly blocks together into six horizontal rows with five butterflies in each row and yellow vertical sashing strips between the blocks. Press the seams toward the sashes.

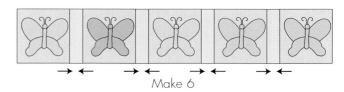

Make 6

Trim the pieced horizontal sashing strips to the exact *length* of the rows. Sew the horizontal sashing strips between the butterfly rows, being careful to line up the vertical sashes. Press toward the sashes.

Piece blue print inner border strips with diagonal seams pressed open. (See page 19 for instruction on measuring and sewing borders.) Measure and cut two borders the same length as the horizontal sashing strips. Before sewing the top and bottom borders to the quilt, measure and cut two side borders the *length* of the quilt. Sew the top and bottom borders to the quilt. Press toward the borders.

Add the yellow cornerstones cut earlier to both ends of the side borders of the quilt. Press toward the blue borders. Sew to the sides of the quilt. Press toward the borders.

Using the white border strips cut earlier, measure and cut borders for the top and bottom of the quilt. Sew to the quilt. Press toward the borders.

In the same manner, add borders to the sides of the quilt. Press toward the borders.

Finishing the Quilt
Mark any quilting designs on the quilt top before layering. Layer, baste, and quilt. This quilt was marked in a diagonal 1" grid in each of the blocks. The butterflies were out-line-quilted, and also quilting was done along the embroidery lines in the butterflies. The yellow sashes were hand-quilted with a small cable, and the inner blue border was quilted in a differ-ent cable design. The wide outer border was quilted with a curving feather design.

Binding
Before binding, hand or machine baste a scant 1/4" from the edge of the quilt. This will prevent the lay-ers from shifting while the binding is being sewn on. Cut 2¼" bias strips from the blue print fabric. Join with diagonal seams pressed open. Fold wrong sides together and press. Sew to the

quilt with a ¼" seam, mitering the corners. (See page 21 for instruction on binding). Trim the excess batting and backing, then turn the binding to the back side of the quilt and stitch down by hand with matching thread.

Design Options

❖ Set the butterflies on point (on the diagonal) in each block, then set the blocks on point either with sashing or alternate print blocks.
❖ Set the blocks together as shown, but use smaller blocks and wider sashing.
❖ Use 2½" squares of the prints matching the butterflies to make scrappy sashings, and set the blocks and sashing as shown or on point.
❖ Instead of wide plain borders, add a border of butterflies after the first print border. Add a second border after the butterfly border.
❖ Arrange the butterflies so they fly out in all directions from the center. Then, no matter where your position, at least some butterflies will be right side up.

However you arrange your butterflies, don't forget to sign and date your Butterfly quilt!

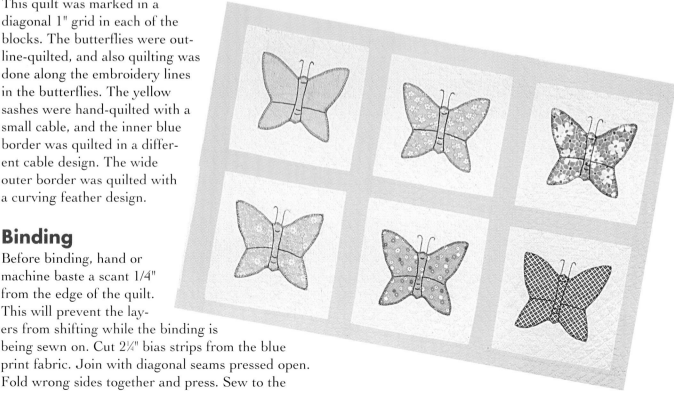

Butterfly template

Vintage top hand quilted by author.

Bride's Bouquet

Bride's Bouquet

This charming block, alternately called Nosegay, was very popular in the 1930s. Who wouldn't love it … a pattern so reminiscent of an old-fashioned June bride? I found this quilt top at a local estate auction, and immediately fell in love with it. As I was hand quilting it, this is the story it whispered in my ear …

Mama got married at the height of the Great Depression. Money was scarce for everyone, but farmers at least had their own homegrown vegetables and fruits, meat, eggs, and milk, and could get by. Somehow money was found to buy the fabric for Mama's dress, and they planned to use garden flowers for the simple church wedding. All the preparations were made, but Grandma insisted Mama should make a wedding quilt. Grandma suggested her favorite pattern for a wedding quilt: Rose of Sharon, but Mama wanted the new-fangled pattern she found in a magazine, called Nosegay or Bride's Bouquet.

With the "make do or do without" philosophy of the time, the scrap bag was called into service. The scrap bag contained a wonderful variety of fabrics: all the leftover pieces from making aprons and dresses. Some of the pieces were from feedsacks, the sacks that flour, sugar, and chicken feed came in. Mama chose all the bright colorful bits, while Grandma found a solid blue piece large enough for all the "vases" in the blocks. The plain background came from white feedsacks. Mama had to bleach them and lay them out in the sun to remove all the printing. (Look carefully; you can still see faint printing on some of the muslin.) Mama happily began to piece the blocks, but Grandma fretted over what to use for sashings and borders: it would take a number of yards of the same fabric for that purpose. Finally, she remembered the eight yards of curtain lining material she had packed away in the cedar chest. It would be perfect (although rather lightweight) when dyed a soft, butter yellow.

When Mama announced she was tired of making blocks, the quilt was laid out and wide sashes and borders were cut from Grandma's newly dyed curtain lining to help make the quilt large enough. A quilting bee with all the neighbor women was held to get it finished in time for the wedding. Mama always treasured this quilt (her first!) and saved it for the best bed when company came.

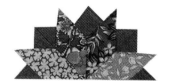  

Tool Requirements

Companion Angle
Easy Eight (optional)

Fabric Requirements

Blue solid: ½ yd.
Green solid: ½ yd.
White: 3½ yd.
Prints: A variety of scraps totaling 2 yd.
Yellow solid: 4⅔ yd.
Backing: 8½ yd.

Cutting Directions (for new version)

This quilt is made up of 25 blocks, six of which have been cut in half and used at the top and bottom, or at the sides. One block has been cut in quarters; part used in the top left corner, and another part used in the bottom right.

Notice the quilt is square, and it isn't symmetrical. You may choose to follow the original, or with the same number of blocks make the quilt symmetrical. The updated version would have empty side and corner triangles to showcase a lovely quilting design. (See graphic page 67 of re-vamped design.)

Note: You may choose to cut your border strips the length of the fabric before cutting your sashing strips. Cut the strips a few inches longer than needed.

From	Cut	To Yield
Green solid	7 – 2¼" strips	125 – 2¼" squares
White	5 – 2¼" strips	75 – 2¼" squares
	8 – 2¼" strips	75 – 2¼" x 4" rectangles
	5 – 1¾" strips	100 Companion Angle triangles
	3 – 23" strips	3 – 23" squares, cut twice on the diagonal for setting triangles
		2 – 13" squares, cut once on the diagonal for corner triangles
		25 Template A
		25 Template A reversed
Blue solid		25 Template A
		25 Template A reversed
Variety of prints	3" strips	Cut 150 diamonds with Easy Eight or template page 69
Yellow solid	5 – 12½" strips	64 sashing strips 3" x 12½"
	4 – 3" strips*	40 squares for cornerstones*
	9 – 5½" strips	Border
	2¼" bias strips	Binding

Consider using a different color or print for the cornerstones.

Note: If not using Companion Angle, cut 25 – 3¾" squares, cut twice on the diagonal. If not using Easy Eight, use the template on page 69.

Note: The white half blocks are larger than needed and will be trimmed later.

Assembling the Blocks

Assemble the corner units of green and white. Join the two squares and press toward the green square. Add the rectangle to one side to form a square. Press toward the rectangle.

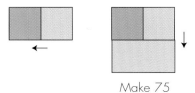

Make 75

Assemble the triangle units that fit between the points. Make 50. Sew a white triangle to the right side of a green square. Press toward the green square. Add a white triangle to the left adjacent side of the square. Press toward the triangle. Trim off the dog-ears.

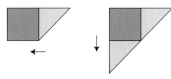

Sew a triangle unit to the right side of a diamond. Sew up to ¼" from the corner, then stop, and backstitch. Sew another diamond to the adjacent side of the triangle unit. Stop and backstitch ¼" from the corner. Starting at the seam allowance and back-stitching, sew the seam joining the two diamonds. Press all the seams to the left. Repeat this procedure for one more diamond/triangle unit.

Sew a pieced square to the right side of a diamond/triangle unit, sewing to within ¼" from the corner, and then back-stitching. Add another diamond/triangle unit in the same manner to the adjacent side of the pieced square. Sew the seam between the two diamond units. Press the center seam open.

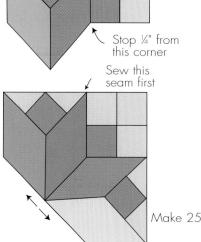

Sew a diamond to the shortest edge of the blue A piece. Stop and backstitch ¼" from the corner as before. Set in the A (reversed) white piece. Press. Repeat this procedure for the mirror image of this unit using blue A (reversed) and white A.

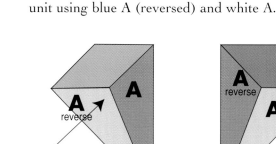

Sew the seam joining the two blue pieces. Press this seam open.

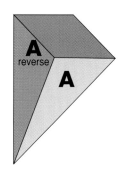

Make 25

Sew the top pieced unit to the bottom vase unit, stopping ¼" in from the edges. Press this seam open. Set in the remaining pieced square units. Repeat to make a total of 25 blocks.

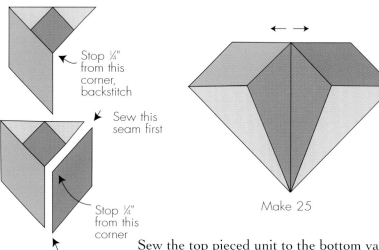

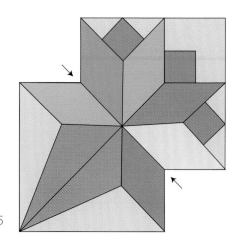

Make 25

Assembling the Quilt Top

Lay out the blocks and half blocks on point to match

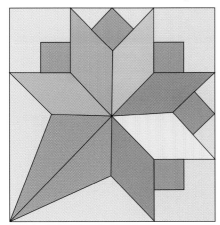

Make 25 blocks

the photograph of the quilt, or match the graphic of the quilt in the new arrangement. Join the pieced blocks, the setting triangles, and yellow sashing strips in diagonal rows.

Note: The white setting triangles are larger than needed and will be trimmed later.

Press toward the sashing.

Sew the sashing and cornerstones together in rows. Press toward the sashing strips.

Join the rows of blocks with the rows of sashing and cornerstones. Press all the seams toward the sashing.

Trimming the Quilt Top

The edges of the quilt top are now trimmed to square up the quilt.

Press the entire top, then on a large flat surface, lay out as much of the quilt as possible. With a long ruler, lightly mark a cutting line to trim the quilt edges, leaving ¼" seam allowance from the corners of the cornerstone squares. Keep the edge of the quilt straight, and the corners square. When satisfied the markings are correct, go back and trim on those markings.

Borders

Trim two 5½" borders to the width of the quilt. Sew these to the top and bottom of the quilt. (See page 19 for instruction on adding borders.) Press the seams toward the border. Measure and cut as before and add the side borders to the quilt. Press toward the borders.

Finishing

Mark any quilting designs on the quilt top. Layer and baste the quilt sandwich.

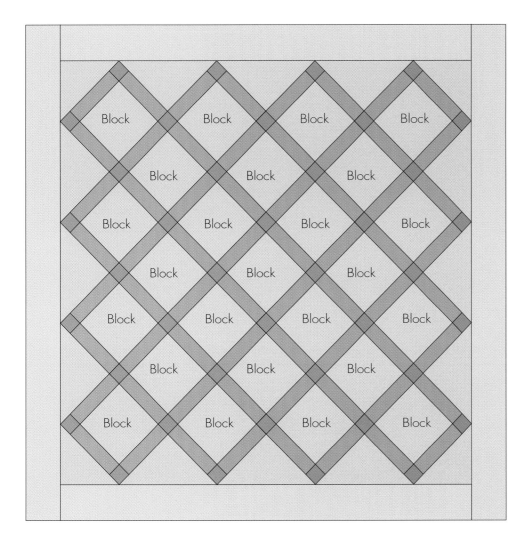

The quilt shown was hand quilted "by the piece," that is, ¼" from the seam allowances in the blocks. A pretty flower motif was quilted in the wide sashes and also in the border.

Binding

Before binding, hand or machine baste (with a walking foot) close to the edge of the quilt. Do not trim off excess batting and backing yet.

Cut double bias binding strips at 2¼". Join with diagonal seams pressed open. Press the binding in half, right sides out. Sew the binding to the quilt top with a ¼" seam allowance. Trim off excess batting and backing, and turn the binding to the back side of the quilt. Stitch the binding down by hand with matching thread, being careful not to let your stitches come through to the front of the quilt. (See page 21 for instruction on binding.)

Sign your quilt and enjoy!

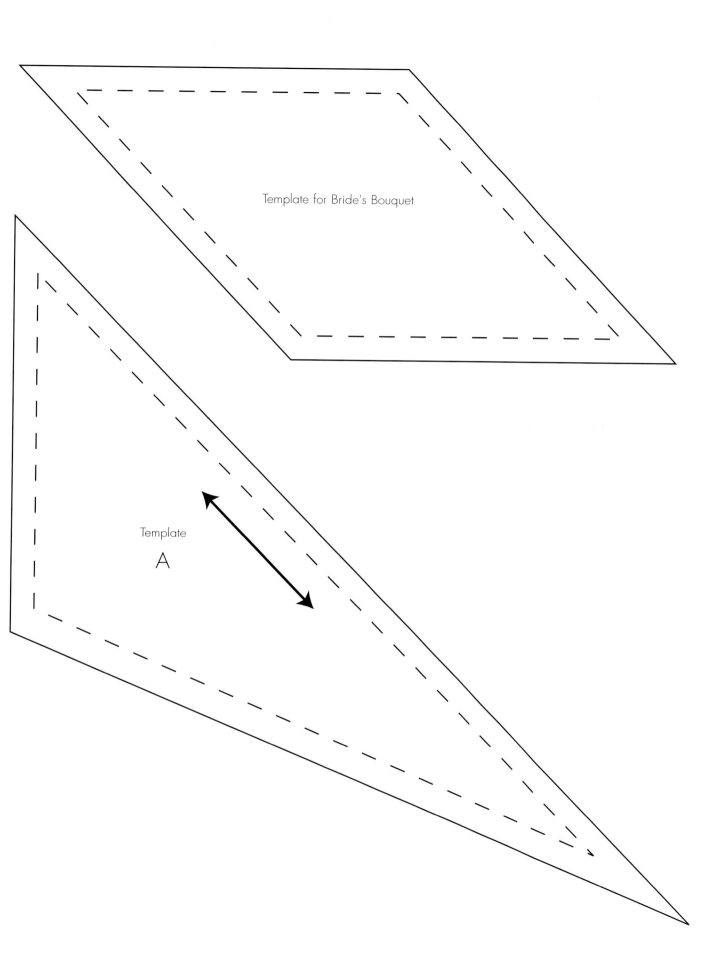

Template for Bride's Bouquet

Template

A

Vintage top hand quilted by author.

Sweet Memories

This is a combination new/vintage quilt. The center square section and the pieced corner sections were discovered in an antique shop in Minnesota. The sections were color coordinated, carefully and precisely pieced, and all the seams were pressed open. However, there was no further indication of what the original quiltmaker had intended to do with the pieces! I decided to set the center square on point, followed by a white border and the pieced corners to finish out the quilt. Before the sections were put together, pink triangles were added to frame the pieces. The white border was the perfect open area to add appliquéd flowers and leaves, which were cut from vintage fabrics. The narrow striped border on the outer edge helped to separate the busy prints in the quilt from the prairie point border, which continued the theme of the pink triangles framing the sections. It was a very enjoyable project to work on, and quite satisfying to take the five ordinary quilt sections and turn them into something pretty.

You can re-create this vintage beauty using reproduction prints or even some of your vintage feedsack or dress goods fabric! This would be a wonderful place to showcase those special fabrics.

Quilt shown is 60" square

Fabric Requirements

Variety of prints: 2½ yd. total
Pink solid: 1⅛ yd.
White or off-white background: 1⅔ yd.
Green check for leaves: ¼ yd.
Pink stripe: ⅜ yd.
Backing: 3¾ yd.

Cutting Directions

From	Cut	To Yield
Variety of prints	2¾" strips	364 – 2¾" squares
	14 – 4½" squares, cut twice diagonally	56 triangles
White	4 – 5¼" x 47" strips cut lengthwise (for borders)	
	3 – 3½" strips	28 – 3½" squares, cut twice diagonally to make 112 triangles
		2 – 3⅛" squares, cut once diagonally to make 4 corner triangles
Pink solid	3 – 3½" strips	28 – 3½" squares cut twice diagonally to make 112 triangles.
	8 – 3" strips	100 – 3" squares (for prairie points)
Pink stripe	6 – 1¾" strips	Border

Assembling the Center and Corner Units

Sew together a variety of 14 print squares in a row. Make 14 rows. Press the seams in each row one direction, alternating the direction in every other row. Sew the rows together. At this point, the square should measure 32" unfinished.

Sew together 14 pink triangles and 13 white triangles on the short edges to make a strip as shown. *Do not press!* To prevent stretching, sew the pieced borders to the quilt center *before* pressing. Pin at each seam intersection. After sewing, press the

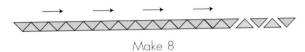

Make 8

seams all one direction. Make eight of these units, setting four aside to be used for the corners. Add the white corner triangles last.

Assemble four corner units as shown, using a variety of 42 print squares and 14 print triangles for each corner unit. Press the corner unit.

Add white triangles to both ends of each of the remaining four pink/white triangle border strips.

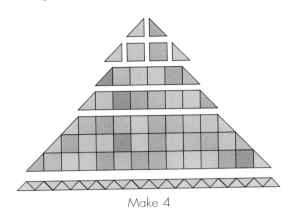

Make 4

Sew to the long edge of each of the pieced corner units. Press the seams toward the pieced units.

Using the white borders cut earlier, trim two of the borders the exact width of the quilt. Sew to the top and bottom of the square. Press toward the borders.

Trim the remaining two borders the length of the quilt. Sew to the sides of the quilt. Press toward the white borders.

Sew the corner units to the sides of the quilt center square. Mark and match the centers of the quilt square and the corners. *The white borders will extend beyond the corner units.* Trim the excess white border off evenly with the pieced border corners.

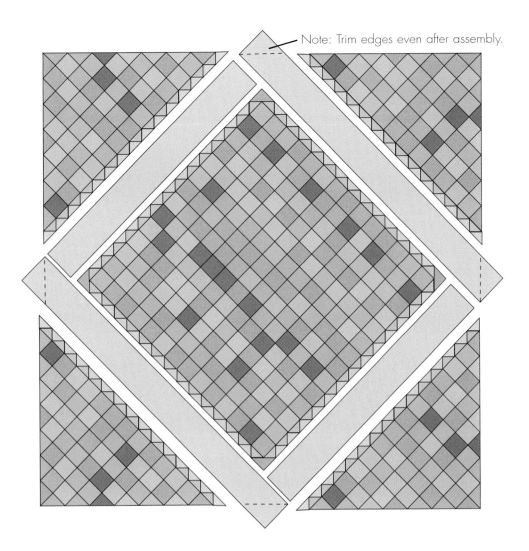

Note: Trim edges even after assembly.

Borders

Measure, cut, and piece two 1¾" pink stripe borders the exact width of the quilt. Sew to the top and bottom of the quilt. Press the seams toward the border. (See page 19 for instruction on adding borders.) Measure, cut and piece 2 borders the exact length of the quilt. Sew to the sides of the quilt. Press the seams toward the border.

Appliqué

Using the templates given on page 74, trace 16 flowers, 16 flower centers and 32 leaves on the dull side of freezer paper. Cut out on the marked line. With a warm iron, press the freezer paper templates to the wrong side of the fabrics chosen for the appliqué. Cut out, adding a scant ¼" seam allowance. Clip any inside corners or curves. Finger-press or with a warm iron, turn the seam allowances over the edge of the freezer paper. You can remove the paper before or after stitching. (See pages 18-19 for appliqué instruction and options.) Using the picture as a guide, center the flowers and leaves on the white borders. Appliqué in place with a blind stitch and matching thread.

Edging

Prepare each of the 3" pink solid squares for the prairie points. Fold in half on the diagonal, then in half again. Tuck one end inside the previous one to make a continuous border. There are 25 prairie points on each side of the quilt. Adjust the prairie point border to fit the quilt. Sew the prairie points onto the striped border with a ¼" seam.

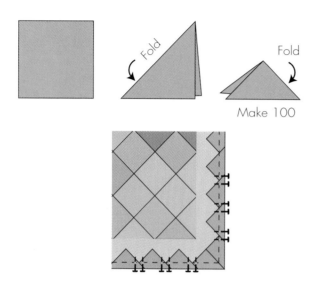

Make 100

Finishing the Quilt

Cut backing and batting several inches larger than the quilt top. Layer, baste, and quilt. The pieced center and corner units were hand quilted in the ditch on each seam line, and through the middle of the square in each direction. The appliqué in the white border was outline-stitched, and then cross-hatching was quilted in the white areas, marked in a diagonal grid from pink point to opposite pink point. *Leave the striped border unquilted for now.*

Trim the excess *batting* the exact size of the quilt top. Trim the excess *backing* ½" larger than the quilt top. Turn and press prairie points to the outside of the quilt. Turn the backing over ½" and covering the stitching line on the back of the quilt, hand stitch the backing to the back side of the quilt.

After the edge has been finished, you can go back and quilt the striped border.

Sign and date your quilt so future generations will know who made it!

Flower Template for Sweet Memories

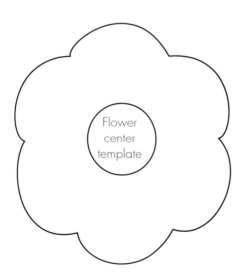

Flower center template

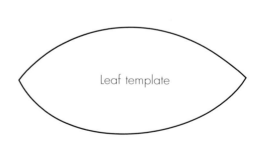

Leaf template

Sweet Memories

Reproduction fabrics, pieced and machine quilted by author, hand quilting by Pam Kienholz.

Aunt Maggie's Quilt

T his sweet quilt with stars dancing across the surface is a charmer from the past. Job's Tears and Periwinkle are two of the traditional names for this quilt block. However, in the original pattern the pieces have to be cut with templates, and there are many set-in seams. This quilt, with its updated method of construction, allows the pieces to be rotary cut and simply pieced. The setting has changed also – the stars are set with sashing, but additional stars are pieced into the sashing to fit the stars closer together. You'll need to make star blocks and partial star blocks to set into the pieced sashing. The crowning touch is a mock ice-cream cone border.

To make this quilt bed-size, I've written directions for making the *block* larger. The construction is the same, but it finishes larger.

Quilt shown: 62" x 70", 6" block, 7 x 8 setting
Larger size: 93" x 105", 9" block, 7 x 8 setting

Tool Requirements

Tri-Recs
Companion Angle
Easy Angle

Fabric Requirements

White: 3¾ yd. (6⅔ yd.)
Assorted prints: 24 fat eighths or ⅛ yd.; 3½ yd. total;
   (⅜ yd. of 24 prints or 9¼ yd. total)
Print for border: 1⅛ yd. (2¼ yd.)
Backing: 3⅔ yd. (8¼ yd.)

Cutting Directions for Lap Quilt (6" block)

From	Cut	To Yield
White	19 – 2½" strips	295 squares
	20 – 2½" strips	396 pairs of Recs triangles*
	3 – 2½" strips	26 rectangles 2½" x 4½"
	5 – 2½" strips	116 Tri triangles (for pieced border)
	6 – 1½" strips	116 Companion Angle triangles (for pieced border)
		4 Easy Angle triangles (for pieced border)
From each print	1 – 2½" x 42" strip**	22 Tri triangles
	1 – 1½" x 42" strip**	22 Companion Angle triangles
Print for border	8 – 2" strips	Inside border
	1 – 3½" strip	4 squares for border corners
	7 – 2¼" strips	Binding

*Leave fabric strips folded and you will automatically cut pairs.
** Cut 2 strips if using fat eighths.

Cutting Directions for Queen-Size Quilt (9" block)

From	Cut	To Yield
White	26 – 3½" strips	295 squares
	25 – 3½" strips	396 pairs of Recs triangles*
	5 – 3½" strips	26 rectangles 3½" x 6½"
	7 – 3½" strips	116 Tri triangles (for pieced border)
	7 – 2" strips	116 Companion Angle triangles (for pieced border)
		4 Easy Angle triangles (for pieced border)
Assorted prints	2 – 3½" strips	22 Tri triangles
	2 – 2" strips	22 Companion Angle triangles
Print for border	11 – 3" strips	Inside border
	1 – 5" strip	4 squares for border corners
	2¼" bias strips	Binding

*Leave fabric strips folded and you will automatically cut pairs.

Note: If not using Companion Angle, cut four – 3¼" (4¼") squares from each fabric, cut twice on the diagonal. There is no substitute for the Tri-Recs tools. If not using Easy Angle, cut $1^7/_8$" ($2^3/_8$") squares, cut once on the diagonal.

Star Block Assembly

(Make 56 whole blocks, 42 partial blocks)

Note: The pieces left over after assembling your blocks will be used in the pieced border.

Choose two coordinating prints for each star. Assemble two Tri-Recs units of two prints. (See instruction on page 124 for piecing Tri-Recs units.) Press the seams out.

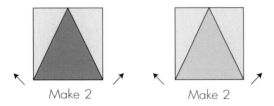

Make 2   Make 2

Using the same two fabrics, sew two pairs of Companion Angle triangles, keeping the same print on top each time. Press this seam open.

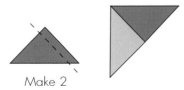

Make 2

Join to make a *Broken Dishes* unit. Press this seam open.

Assemble a block from the units. Follow the pressing directions.

Assemble a total of 56 whole blocks.

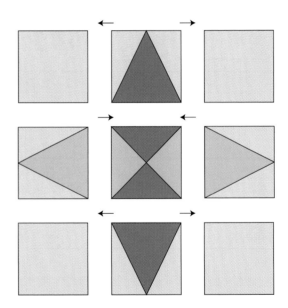

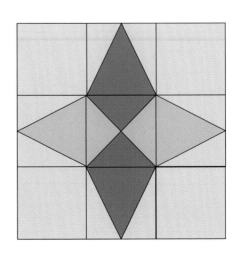

Also assemble the units for 42 more blocks, but stop when you reach this point. (These will be the stars in the sashing.)

 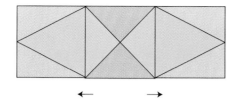

Quilt Assembly

Lay out several rows of your quilt, leaving space between your blocks for the sashings. Add your partial blocks and the white squares and rectangles as the sashings. Lay out the quilt in sections to arrange the colors properly.

Assemble the vertical sashing strips first. Press as shown.

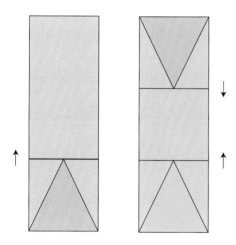

Join the blocks and vertical sashing strips to form 8 rows with 7 complete stars in each row. Press as shown.

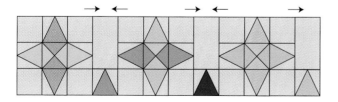

Assemble the horizontal sashing rows. Press as shown.

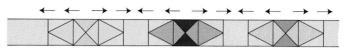

Join all the rows, matching at the seam intersections. Press the seam allowances toward the sashing rows.

Borders

Add the narrow border to the quilt. (See page 19 for instruction on adding borders.)
This border is probably wider than needed, and can be trimmed to make the pieced border fit.

Pieced Border

Piece 28 print Tri triangles and 27 white Tri triangles for the top and bottom border, alternating print and white. End each border row with a white

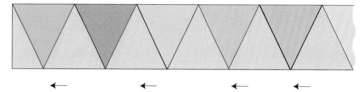

Recs triangle to make a square corner. Press the seams all one direction.
Assemble the top of the ice cream cones with print triangles alternated with white triangles. Match the top of the cones to the bottoms. Begin and end each row with an Easy Angle triangle for a square corner.

Do not press this section, it might stretch.

TIP: Make sure you have a ¼" seam allowance from the tips of the print and white triangles.

Sew the two pieced border sections together, matching and pinning where the seams have to meet. Press the top section all one direction. Press the joining seam open. Make two pieced borders for the top and bottom of the quilt.

Piece 32 print Tri triangles and 31 white Tri tri-

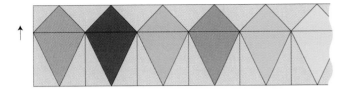

angles for the side borders as before. Add white Recs triangles at both ends to make a square corner. Press the seams all one direction.

Piece print and white small triangles to make the top of the ice cream cones as before. Sew the two parts of the side border strips together and press the seam open.

To make the pieced border fit the quilt top exactly, trim the **_width_** of the quilt top evenly to match the length of the pieced top and bottom borders. **_Do not sew to the quilt top yet!_**

Trim the **_length_** of the quilt top evenly to match the length of the side pieced borders. Add the print corner squares to both ends of the side pieced borders.

Sew the top and bottom pieced borders to the quilt. Press the seams toward the narrow border. Sew the side pieced borders to the sides of the quilt. Press the seams toward the narrow border.

Finishing the Quilt

Mark any quilting design on the quilt before layering. Layer, baste, and quilt. The quilt shown was machine meandered in all the white areas, and hand stitched ¼" from the seams in all the stars and the ice cream cones in the border. Stitching was done on both sides of the narrow border, and a design quilted in the corner squares.

Binding

Before binding, hand or machine baste (with a walking foot) a scant ¼" from the edge of the quilt. This will prevent the layers from shifting while the binding is being sewn on. Prepare the double-fold binding (see page 21 for binding instructions). Sew to the quilt with ¼" seam. Trim the excess batting and backing, and turn the binding to the back side of the quilt. Stitch down by hand with matching thread.

Sign and date your special quilt!

Aunt Maggie's Quilt

Newly created with reproduction fabrics. Machine pieced and quilted by author.

Lemon Twist

T his quilt gives a refreshing new twist on some perennial favorites: the four-patch and the nine-patch. The clean, sunshine yellow and the gorgeous, deep sky-blue pair up with scraps in a simple variation of a star block. The nine-patch and four-patch blocks are connected with yellow rectangles with blue corners added. The simple addition of the blue corners makes stars suddenly appear around the four-patches and gives the quilt a latticework effect. Easy enough for a beginner to piece; but an exciting pattern in any combination of colors!

Quilt shown: 52" x 62", 5 x 6 setting
Larger size: 96" x 106", 9 x10 setting

Fabric Requirements

Variety of prints: 11(22) ¼ yd. (can be fat quarters)
Dark blue solid: 2½ yd.(5¾ yd.)
Light yellow solid: 1½ yd.(4 yd.)
Backing: 3¼ yd.(8½ yd.)

Cutting Directions

From	Cut	To Yield
Yellow solid	9(27) – 4½" strips	49(161) – 4½" x 6½" rectangles
	3(5) – 2½" strips	22(38) – 2½" x 4½" rectangles
Blue solid	15(45) – 2½" strips	240(720) – 2½" squares
	2(5) – 2½" strips	5(18) – 2½" x 10½" rectangles
	7(11) – 2½" (4½") strips	Border
	2¼" bias strips	Binding
Each print	2(3) – 2½" x 42" strips	8(12) – 2½" x 10½" rectangles

Nine-Patch Blocks

Make 20 (72)

Sew three different print rectangles (2½" x 10½") together on their long edges to make Strip Set A. Make 15(45) different strip sets. Press as indicated. Cut into 58(178) – 2½" x 6½" units.

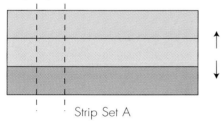

Strip Set A

Sew two different print rectangles on either side of one blue solid rectangle to make Strip Set B. Make 5(18) different strip sets. Press toward the blue strip. Cut into 20(72) – 2½" x 6½" units.

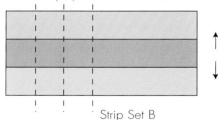

Strip Set B

Join two Strip Set A units and one Strip Set B unit to make a nine-patch block. Press toward the center strip. Make 20(72) nine-patch blocks. Reserve the remainder of the Strip Set A units for outside edges.

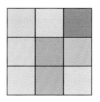

Four-Patch Blocks

Make 30 (90)

Sew two different print rectangles together to make Strip Set C. Make 15(45) different strip sets. (You will have three strips left over.) Press. Cut into 60(180) – 2½" x 4½" units. Join two different units to make 30(90) four-patch blocks. Press this seam open.

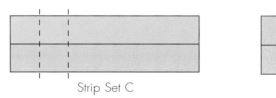

Strip Set C

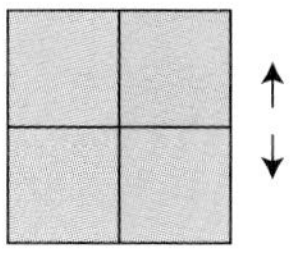

Connecting Blocks

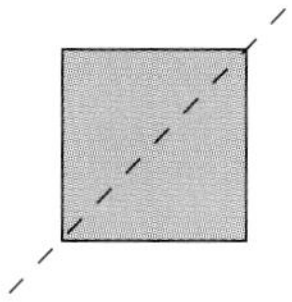

Make 49 (161)

Mark a diagonal line on the wrong side of all the blue solid squares. Place a blue square on a corner of a 4½" x 6½" yellow rectangle as shown. Stitch on the line. Trim the seam allowance to ¼", and press the seam toward the blue triangle. Repeat on all four corners.

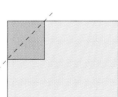

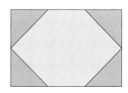

Granny Quilts 83

Repeat this procedure on the corners of the yellow 2½" x 4½" rectangles. Make 22(38).

Assembling the Quilt

Join 5(9) four-patches, 4(8) yellow/blue connecting blocks, and two yellow/blue rectangles to make Block Row A. Press toward the four-patches. Make 6(10) rows.

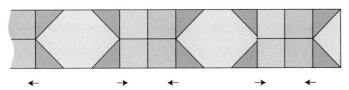

Join 4(8) nine-patch blocks, 5(9) yellow/blue connecting blocks, and two Strip Set A units to make Block Row B. Press toward the nine-patches. Make 5(9) rows.

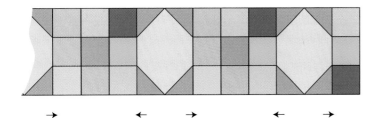

Join 4(8) Strip Set A's, 5(9) yellow/blue rectangles, and two print squares to make Block Row C. Press toward the Strip Set A's. Make 2 rows.

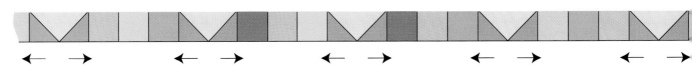

Join the rows as shown in the quilt photo. Press the seams toward the nine-patch rows.

Borders

Join the border strips with diagonal seams pressed open. Measure and cut two borders the width of the quilt top. (See page 19 for instructions on adding borders.) Sew to the quilt top. Press toward the borders.

Add the side borders in the same manner.

Finishing the Quilt

Mark any quilting designs on the quilt top. Layer, baste, and quilt. The quilt shown was machine meandered in all the print squares and yellow areas. A simple cable border was quilted in the border.

Binding

Before binding, hand or machine baste a scant ¼" from the edges of the quilt. This will keep the layers from shifting while the binding is being sewn on.

Prepare the blue solid binding (See page 21 for instruction on binding) and sew to the quilt with a ¼" seam. Trim excess batting and backing, turn to the back side and stitch down by hand with matching thread.

Sign and date your special quilt!

Lemon Twist

Reproduction fabrics, pieced and machine quilted by author.

Cabin in the Spring

Inspired by an antique quilt in my collection, I created the same Log Cabin design in reproduction fabrics. The Log Cabin block originated around the time of the Civil War and was associated with Abraham Lincoln and his campaign claim that he grew up in a log cabin. The narrow rectangles that make up the block certainly remind one of the logs making up a cabin. Traditionally, the center square was red to signify the hearth or the heart of the home. Usually seen in the dark indigoes, Turkey reds, mourning grays and shirtings of the mid- to late 1800s, the Log Cabin design takes on a completely different look in the soft pastels of the '30s.

To make this quilt, you'll need to find light reproduction fabrics for the light half of the block; use darker prints for the other half. The color differences are subtle, so keep the fabrics separate and labeled to prevent confusion.

The construction is very easy; unlike most Log Cabins, cut the pieces the exact size you need. No need to trim after each addition and the blocks stay square.

Fabric Requirements

12(25) light prints or prints with white backgrounds: ¼ yd. of each
6(12) green prints: ¼ yd. of each
Green print for block centers: ⅛ yd.
5(9) blue prints: ¼ yd. of each
4 lavender prints: ⅛ yd. of each (¼ yd. of each)
Yellow print: ⅛ yd.
Pink print for centers: ⅔ yd.(1¼ yd.)
Binding: ⅝ yd. (1 yd.)
Backing: 3½ yd. (8⅓ yd.)

Note: Fat quarters can be substituted for quarter yards. You will need to cut twice as many strips as called for in the cutting table to yield the proper number of pieces.

Cutting Directions

From	Cut	To Yield
Pink print	5(10) – 4" strips	44(96) – 4" squares for centers
Green print	1 – 4" strip	4 squares for centers
Yellow print	1 – 2¼" strip	16 squares for centers
Each light print	4 – 1½" strips	4 – 1½" x 4"
		4 – 1½" x 5"
		4 – 1½" x 6"
		4 – 1½" x 7"
		4 – 1½" x 8"
		4 – 1½" x 9"
Each green print	5 – 1½" strips	4 – 1½" x 5"
		4 – 1½" x 6"
		4 – 1½" x 7"
		4 – 1½" x 8"
		4 – 1½" x 9"
		4 – 1½" x 10"
Each blue print	5 – 1½" strips	4 – 1½" x 5"
		4 – 1½" x 6"
		4 – 1½" x 7"
		4 – 1½" x 8"
		4 – 1½" x 9"
		4 – 1½" x 10"
Each lavender print	2(5) – 1½" strips	1(4) – 1½" x 5"
		1(4) – 1½" x 6"
		1(4) – 1½" x 7"
		1(4) – 1½" x 8"
		1(4) – 1½" x 9"
		1(4) – 1½" x 10"
Binding	2¼" bias strips	Double bias binding

Block Assembly

Make four pieced center squares using the green 4"
squares and the yellow 2¼" squares. Mark a diagonal
line on the back side of the yellow squares. Place a
square on one corner of the green square and sew
from corner to corner. Trim the seam to ¼", and
press toward the green square. Repeat at all four
corners. Make four pieced center squares.

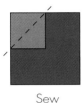  

Sew   Trim   Make 4

Using one of the pieced center
squares, sew a 1½" x 4" light rectangle to the top of the square.
Press toward the
rectangle.

Sew a 1½" x 5" light rectangle
to the right side of the unit.
Press toward the piece just
added.

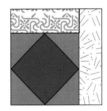

Turn the block a quarter
turn to the left. Sew a
1½" x 5" lavender print
rectangle to the right side
of the unit. Press toward
the lavender rectangle.

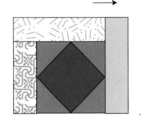

Turn the block a quarter
turn to the left again.
Sew a 1½" x 6" *different*
lavender print rectangle
to the right side of the
unit. Press toward the
lavender rectangle.

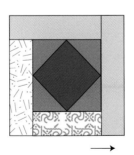

Repeat, using light and lavender rectangles until the
block measures 10" square. Repeat to make four
lavender blocks with pieced center squares.

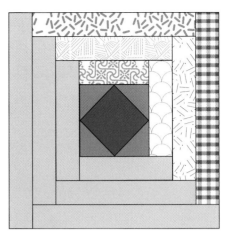

Using the pink center squares for the remainder of
the blocks and following the directions above, make
the required number of blocks in each color.

Lap-Size (48 blocks)   **Queen Size** (100 blocks)
4 lavender blocks   16 lavender blocks
20 blue blocks   36 blue blocks
24 green blocks   48 green blocks

Assembling the Quilt

Lay out the blocks in any arrangement, or the one
shown in the photo. Sew the blocks together in
rows, pressing the seams all one direction in each
even numbered row, and the opposite way in
uneven numbered rows.

Sew the rows together, pinning and matching seam
allowances. Press all the seams the same direction.

Queen Size Cabin in the Spring

Finishing the Quilt

Mark any quilting designs on the quilt top. Layer, baste, and quilt. The quilt shown was machine quilted in a large meander over the surface of the quilt, with a cloverleaf design quilted in the large center squares.

Before binding, hand or machine baste (use a walking foot) a scant ¼" from the edge of the quilt. This will prevent the layers from shifting while the binding is being sewn on.

Cut bias strips for binding. (See page 21 for instructions on binding.) Piece with diagonal seams pressed open. Fold in half, wrong sides together and press. Sew to the quilt with a ¼" seam. Trim excess batting and backing. Turn binding to the back side and stitch down by hand using matching thread and a blind stitch.

Sign and date your special creation!

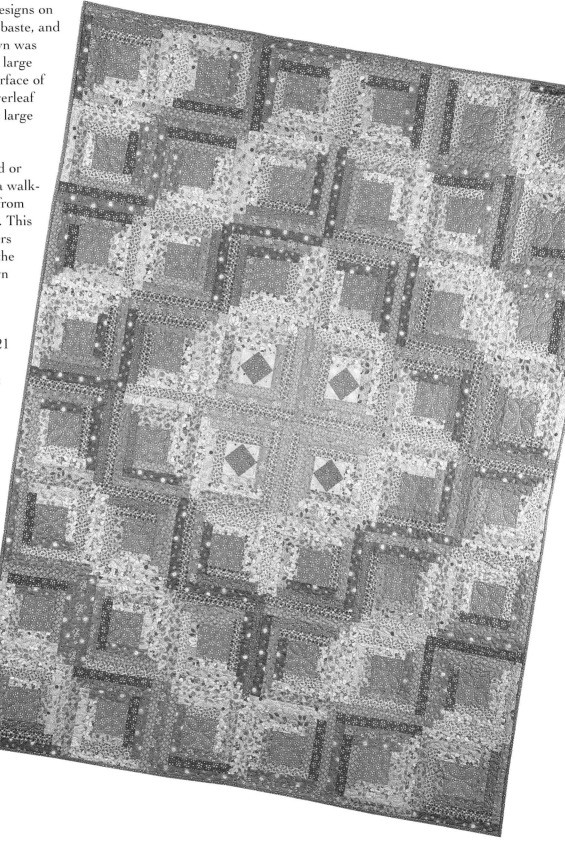

Vintage blocks set together by author, machine quilted by Bonnie Erickson.

Grandmother's Fan

One day in 1935, Anna Mae decided to make a quilt. Seemed like everyone was doing it these days, and now that the children were in school she had a little more free time. She borrowed a Grandmother's Fan pattern from a friend and began her project. The quilt would need lots of white fabric … h'mmm … she had several bed sheets that could be cut up for the background squares. For the prints, why, she had plenty of scraps left from sewing clothes and aprons for herself and the girls! For the background squares, she tore the bed sheet into strips, then squares. With a pencil she carefully traced around the fan template on the back of the print fabrics. Red was her favorite color, so she cut plenty of red. In the evening while listening to the radio and helping the children learn their spelling words, she carefully cut each of the wedges. Finally enough wedges were cut that Anna Mae could piece the 90 fans together on her treadle sewing machine. The red wedges she had cut were carefully placed in the central position in each block. With great difficulty, she pieced the lavender curved fan base to the corner of the fan. Next she needed to attach the fans to the white squares. H'mmm … with no one to show her how, she used quilting thread and, turning the edges over, whipstitched them down. She found it difficult to stitch through the tight weave of the cotton bed sheet!

Finally Anna Mae was ready to set the blocks together, but more problems arose. The blocks weren't fitting together properly, and how could she get them to stand upright as they did on the quilt her friend had shown her? After several failed attempts at sewing the blocks together, she finally gave up, put them all into a box, and put the box in the back of her linen closet. "Someday," she said, "I'll go back to them."

Several years ago I discovered a treasure in an antique shop – an old dress box with many completed fan blocks dating from the 1930s era. It also contained extra fabric, the old templates, and two failed attempts at setting the blocks together.

I took the blocks apart that were set together, re-appliquéd the fans with finer thread, and squared the blocks to the same size (they varied by several inches). I set the lovely blocks together and added reproduction lavender print borders to match the lavender solid in the fan blocks. The lavender should clash with the red wedge in each block, but somehow it works beautifully.

For the quilting, I broke my own golden rule and had the quilt professionally machine-quilted. The experience of hand-appliquéing all those fans had taught me it was too difficult to hand-quilt through the bed sheet fabric. Now that her quilt is finished, I do hope Anna Mae is smiling down at me!

If you'd like to replicate this quilt exactly as shown, use Anna Mae's templates given on page 94 for a fan with seven wedges. Or, you can use the Easy Dresden and your rotary cutter to make a Grandmother's Fan quilt that looks similar, but with much less work! Easy Dresden will cut pieces for a five-bladed fan. If you wish to skip the appliqué step, see pages 126-127 for another method of finishing the edges. Read through the pattern and Design Options (page 94) before making your choices.

Only eight more blocks are needed to add more width for the larger size, as white setting triangles are used in place of half fan blocks. Wider borders are added for extra length and width.

Quilt shown: 73" x 90", 8" blocks, 6 x 8 setting
Larger size: 89" x 95", 7 x 8 setting

Tool Requirements

Large Square
Easy Dresden (Optional)

Fabric Requirements

White: 6¼ yd. (7½ yd.)
Lavender solid: ⅓ yd. or ⅔ yd. (see options in cutting table)
Variety of prints for fan wedges: 4 yd. total
    or: ⅔ yd. of 5 different prints if using Easy Dresden
    or: ⅝ yd. of 7 different prints if using the template
Print for border and binding: 2 yd. (2¾ yd.)
Backing: 5⅓ yd. (8 yd.)

Cutting Directions

From	Cut	To Yield
White	23(25) – 8½" strips	90(98) – 8½" squares
	1(3) – 13" strips	3(7) – 13" squares, cut twice on the diagonal for setting triangles
	1 – 7" strip	2 – 7" squares, cut once on the diagonal for corners
Each print	5 – 4½" strips	90(98) wedges (if using Easy Dresden)
or	4 – 4½" strips	90(98) wedges (if using the template)
Lavender solid	5 – 2" strips	90(98) 2" squares (if using Easy Dresden)
	7 – 3" strips	90(98) 3" squares (if using the template set)
Print for border	9(10) 3"(5½") strips	Borders
	2¼" bias strips	Binding

Fan Blocks

Make 90(98) fan blocks
If using Easy Dresden, you have two different choices for edge finishes (see page 126 for easy folded points). If you have sewn across the top and turned the points, then follow the directions of page 127 for joining the wedges. Five wedges make up a fan. Baste the fans onto a corner of the white squares.

Or, you can opt to do nothing with the top edges of the Easy Dresden wedges. Sew five wedges together edge to edge, then turn the outer rounded curve of the fan under ¼". Baste the fan in place on a corner of the white squares. Appliqué the fans by hand or machine with a neutral thread.

If using the template on page 94, sew seven wedges together on the long edges to make a fan. Finger press or, with a warm iron, turn the top edge under ¼", keeping the curve smooth. Baste the fan in place on a corner of the white squares. Appliqué the fans by hand or machine with a neutral thread. Make 90(98) fans.

Using the template for the fan base from either the Easy Dresden package or from the original template set (given on page 94), cut a number of freezer paper templates. Iron to the wrong side of the lavender squares, fitting the corner of the template into the corner of the square. Note that seam allowances are added to the *curved* edge only! Cut out, adding a scant ¼" seam allowance on the curved edge. Finger press, or with a warm iron, press the seam allowance over the freezer paper template. Baste down over the corner of the fan. Stitch in place by hand or machine with matching thread. Remove the freezer paper.

Note: the background fabric behind the fans can be trimmed away.

Assembling the Quilt Top

Assemble the quilt in diagonal rows. For the smaller quilt, cut seven fan blocks in half for the side edges. When those fan blocks are cut in half on the diagonal, that long edge will be bias. So, before cutting, lightly crease the diagonal of the block where you will be cutting. Stitch close to this fold on *both* sides, being careful not to stretch the block. This will act as stay-stitching to stabilize that bias edge. Use the half fans to finish out the diagonal rows on the side, and use the large white triangles to fill in the edges at the top and bottom. Use the smallest white triangles for the corners.

For the larger size, set the blocks 7 across with 6 blocks in the alternate rows. Do not cut any blocks in half — use the extra white setting triangles instead.

Press the seams in each diagonal row the same direction, changing the direction in the following row so the seams alternate. Sew the rows together. Press all one direction.

Note that there is quite a bit of white space at the top of the quilt, while at the bottom the fan bases touch the edge. To balance the quilt visually, the top edge can be trimmed. I trimmed my quilt top to measure 2½" from the top of the fans. Once all the quilting is added, it won't be noticeable that the quilt blocks have been trimmed at the top.

Borders

Piece the border lengths as needed with diagonal seams pressed open. (See page 19 for instruction on adding borders.) Sew borders to the top and bottom of the quilt. Press toward the borders.

In the same manner, measure, cut then sew borders to the sides of the quilt. Press the seams toward the borders.

Finishing the Quilt

Mark any quilting designs on the quilt top. Layer, baste, and quilt. The quilt shown was professionally machine quilted with a curving feather design above each fan, and a large meander over the remainder of the quilt.

Binding

Before binding, hand or machine baste (use a walking foot) a scant ¼" from the edge of the quilt. This will prevent the layers from shifting while the binding is being sewn on. Prepare the binding (see page 21) and stitch to the quilt with a ¼" seam allowance. Turn to the back side and stitch down with matching thread.

Sign and date your beautiful *Grandmother's Fan* quilt!

Design Options

❖ The fan blocks can be oriented differently. Try different ways to lay out the blocks to find the most pleasing setting.

❖ If you prefer not to cut blocks in half, you can cut three more 13" squares, then cut twice on the diagonal to give you more white setting triangles. Then you can make seven less fan blocks for the smaller size.

❖ You can place the fans on smaller blocks, as small as 6½", to place the fans closer together, with less white space. Of course, this will make the finished measurement of your quilt smaller.

❖ Use the finished point method of finishing the fan wedges. This will give your quilt an entirely different look! Also, those edges do not need to be appliquéd down – just quilt in place – the points can be left loose for a three-dimensional look!

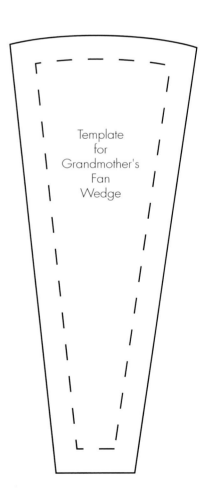

Template for Grandmother's Fan Wedge

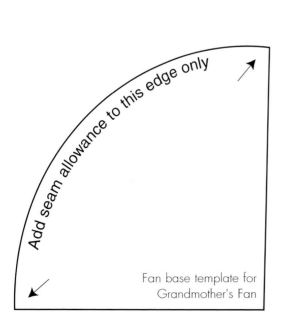

Add seam allowance to this edge only

Fan base template for Grandmother's Fan

Vintage blocks set with reproduction fabric and hand quilted by the author.

Primrose Baskets

The basket blocks were hand pieced in the '30s or '40s by an English woman who settled in North Dakota. When she passed away recently, her family tried to sell this set of blocks for $2 at a garage sale. When they failed to sell, the family gave them to a quilting friend of mine so "they wouldn't feel guilty about not finishing them." My friend, being a professional machine quilter, also didn't have the time to finish them, so sold them to me!

I set the blocks on point adding alternate blocks of reproduction print between the blocks and hand-quilted the top.

This set of blocks was particularly nice because the same fabric was used for all the basket bases (a yellow gingham) and green solid was used in the same position in the baskets, resembling leaves. The "flower" part consists of a variety of prints, including some feedsack fabric.

Quilt shown: 61" x 78½", 6¼" block, 6 x 8 setting
Larger size: 95" x 104", 110 blocks, 10 x 11 setting

Tool Requirements

Easy Angle
Easy Eight (optional)
Companion Angle

Fabric Requirements

White: 1⅔ yd.(3¼ yd.)
Green solid: ⅔ yd.(1⅓ yd.)
Yellow gingham or print: ⅔ yd.(1¼ yd.)
Variety of prints: 2½" x 10" strip for each basket
Light green print: 3¾ yd.(6¼ yd.)
Bright yellow solid: ⅓ yd.(⅜ yd.)
Backing: 3¾ yd.(8¼ yd.)

Cutting Directions

From	Cut	To Yield
White	3(7) – 2½" strips	48(110) – 2½" squares
	6(13) – 1⅞" strips	96(220) Companion Angle triangles
	3(6) – 3½" strips	48(110) Easy Angle triangles
	10(22) – 2" strips	96(220) – 2" x 4" rectangles
Yellow print	3(6) – 3½" strips	48(110) Easy Angle triangles
	4(8) – 2" strips	96(220) Easy Angle triangles
Green solid	9(20) strips*	96(220) – 2" Easy Eight diamonds
Variety of prints	strips*	48(110) pairs of Easy Eight 2" diamonds
Light green print	6(15) – 6¾" strips	35(90) – 6¾" squares
	5(8) – 5½" strips	4 Easy Angle triangles for corners
		24(38) Companion Angle setting triangles
	8(11) – 3½" strips	Outer borders
	2¼" bias strips	Binding
Bright yellow solid	8(11) – 1" strips	Inner borders

*Cut the strips with Easy Eight at the 2" size.

Note: The strip will measure slightly less than 2". Or, use the template for the diamond given on page 99.

If not using Easy Angle, cut 3⅞" squares, 2⅜" squares, and 5⅞" squares respectively. Cut once on the diagonal. If not using Companion Angle, cut 4¼" squares and 11⅞" squares respectively, cut twice on the diagonal.

Basket Block Assembly

Sew a green solid diamond and a print diamond together on one edge as shown. Begin at the *seam allowance*, stitch 2 stitches, then backstitch. Stitch to the edge. Press the seam to the left.

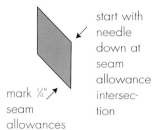 

Sew another green diamond and print diamond together, but reverse their positions. Sew in the same manner, but press the seam to the right. Join the two pairs, starting at the *seam allowance* and stitching to the end. Press this seam open.

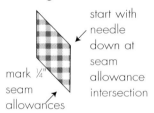

Set in the background squares and triangles as shown. Place the triangle right sides together on top of the green diamond, matching raw edges. Stitch toward the center, stopping when you reach the seam intersection, and backstitch. Press. Repeat to make a total of 48(110) half stars.

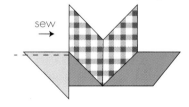

Add the bottom yellow triangle to the top half of the basket. Press toward the yellow triangle. Repeat on all 48(110) blocks.

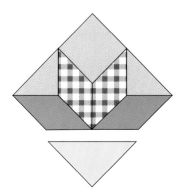

Add small yellow triangles to the white rectangles, making both a right and a left side for the baskets. Make 48(110) for the right side of the basket and 48(110) for the left side of the basket. Press toward the triangles.

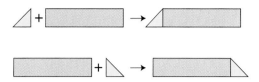

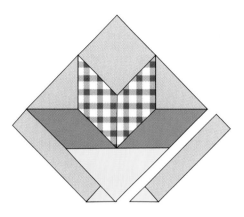

Add these units to the sides of the baskets, pressing toward the strips just added. Add the bottom triangle. Press toward the white triangle. At this point, the blocks should measure 6¾" square, or at least all the same size.

Primrose Baskets

Assembling the Quilt Top

Set the blocks together in diagonal rows, placing plain blocks between the basket blocks, and adding side and corner triangles along the edges. (See flat photo of quilt for layout.) The blocks are set 6(10) across, 8(11) down. Note the setting triangles are slightly larger than needed.

Sew the blocks together in diagonal rows, pressing toward the plain blocks. Sew the block rows together, matching and pinning seam intersections.

Trim the edges of the quilt evenly, leaving at least ¼" seam allowance along the edges.

Borders

Measure, piece, and cut two narrow bright-yellow borders the width of the quilt. (See page 19 for instruction on adding borders.) Sew to the top and bottom of the quilt. Press toward the yellow border. Add the side borders in the same manner.

Measure, cut and piece two print borders the width of the quilt. Sew to the top and bottom of the quilt. Repeat for the side borders.

Finishing the Quilt

Mark any quilting designs on the quilt top. Layer, baste, and quilt. The quilt shown was hand quilted "by the piece" ¼" from the seam lines in the pieced blocks. A pretty design was quilted in the plain alternate blocks. The narrow yellow border was quilted on both sides in the ditch. A tulip motif was quilted in the print border.

Binding

Before binding, hand or machine baste (with a walking foot) a scant ¼" from the edge of the quilt. This will prevent the layers from shifting while the binding is sewn on. Prepare binding (see page 21 for instruction on binding) and sew to the quilt top with a ¼" seam. Trim off excess batting and backing, turn the binding to the back side of the quilt, and stitch down by hand with matching thread.

Sign and date your basket quilt.

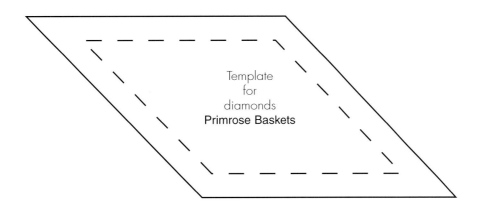

Template
for
diamonds
Primrose Baskets

Antique blocks set with reproduction fabrics, hand-quilted by author.

Lavender Ladies

T his set of antique Colonial Ladies arrived in the mail one day; sent by my friends on the staff at *American Patchwork and Quilting* magazine. They issued a challenge – see what you can do with these! There were 11 blocks in various stages of completion: some were appliquéd and embroidered, others were only appliquéd, and there was a plain square for the twelfth block and a hand-drawn pattern. It didn't take too long to make one more block to complete the set and finish the others. Noticing that all of the ladies were wearing lavender, I chose a lavender reproduction print and framed each of the blocks with lavender solid. I planned to sew it together with only the two lavender fabrics, but found it needed a touch of yellow. Adding yellow star points to the corner-stones was just the spark it needed.

The ladies themselves are a rather crude design, so the pattern given on page 104 is a slightly improved version! Consider using a different block in place of the ladies – an enlarged version of Sunbonnet Sue, a pieced block, or an appliqué block of your choice.

Quilt shown: 64" x 80", 12" block, 3 x 4 setting
Larger size: 96" square, 5 x 5 block setting

Tool Requirement

Large Square
Easy Scallop (optional)

Fabric Requirements

White: 1⅝ yd.(3½ yd.)
Lavender solid: 2½ yd.(3⅓ yd.) (Includes bias binding)
Lavender print for border and sashes: 2½ yd.(3¾ yd.)
Yellow solid: ⅓ yd.(⅝ yd.)
Lavender prints for the ladies: 6" x 10" rectangle for each lady
Backing: 4 yd.(8⅓ yd.)

Other Requirements

Freezer paper or fusible webbing
Black, yellow and 2 shades of lavender embroidery floss
Blue wash-out pen

Cutting Directions

From	Cut	To Yield
White	4(9) – 13" strips	12(25) – 13" squares
Lavender solid	8(17) – 1½" strips	24(50) horizontal sashes 1½" x 12½"
	2(3) – 14½" strips	38(70) vertical sashes 1½" x 14½"
	2 – 1½" strips	18(24) rectangles 1½" x 2½"
		4 – 1½" squares
	2(3) – 2½" strips	20(36) – 2½" squares
	1¼" bias strips	Binding
Lavender print	4 – 6" borders cut lengthwise 84"(100") long	
	31(60) – 2½" x 14½" sashes (cut from remainder of fabric)	
Yellow solid	7(12) – 1½" strips	160(288) – 1½" squares

Block Assembly

Trace the templates on page 104 on the dull side of freezer paper. Cut out on the marked line. Iron to the wrong side of the fabrics chosen for the appliqué. Cut out, adding a scant ¼" seam allowance. (See page 19 for fusible appliqué option.)

Crease the background square from both directions. Transfer the lady design to the fabric square. Use a wash-out pen so the lines can be removed easily after the embroidery is finished. Baste the appliqué pieces in place on the block.

Stitch the appliqué pieces, then finish with embroidery. The lady's body is outlined in black. The flow-ers are stitched with a lazy daisy stitch in two shades of lavender, finished with yellow French knots in the centers.

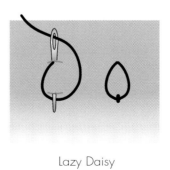

Lazy Daisy

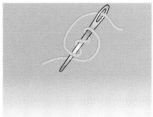

French Knot

When all the embroidery is complete, soak the blocks in cold water to remove the markings. Dry flat. Press, right side down on a bath towel. **Trim to 12½".**

Frame each of the blocks with the solid lavender sashing strips, top and bottom first, sides second. Press seams toward the sashing.

Assembling the Quilt

Assemble 31(60) lavender print sashes as shown below. Mark a diagonal line on the wrong side of all the yellow squares. Place a square on each corner as shown, and stitch on the diagonal line. Trim the seam to ¼" and press toward the yellow triangle.

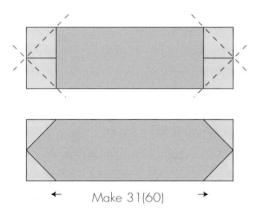

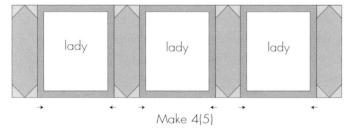

Make 31(60)

Sew 4(5) rows of 3(5) blocks together with the lavender print sashing. Press seams toward the lavender solid sashing.

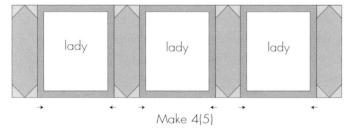

Make 4(5)

Assemble 5(6) rows of horizontal sashing with cornerstones. Press seams toward the cornerstones.

Make 5(6)

Join the rows of blocks and rows of horizontal sashing. Press toward the block rows.

Sew yellow squares onto both corners of the lavender solid rectangles. Trim the seam, and press toward the yellow triangles.

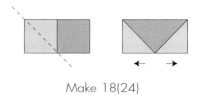

Make 18(24)

Join 4(6) yellow/lavender rectangles and 3(5) long lavender solid sashing strips.. Press as directed. Sew to the top and bottom of the quilt, matching and pinning seam intersections.

Make 2

Join 5(6) yellow/lavender rectangles and 4(5) long lavender solid sashing strips and 2 small lavender solid squares to make the side sashing borders. Press as directed. Sew to the sides of the quilt.

Borders

Measure and trim two lavender print borders the width of the quilt. Sew to the top and bottom of the quilt. Press toward the borders. (See page 19 for instruction on adding borders.)

In the same manner, measure and trim two lavender print borders the length of the quilt. Add to the sides. Press toward the borders.

Finishing the Quilt

Mark any quilting designs, layer, baste, and quilt. The quilt shown was hand quilted in lines radiating out from the center of the lady block. The ladies and the flounces in their dresses were outlined with quilting. The sashing was quilted in the ditch on both sides of the narrow sashing and lines 1½" apart were quilted in the print sashing. The wide outside border was quilted in straight lines 1½" apart.

Binding

The scallops in the border were marked 9½" to 10½" apart. You can use Easy Scallop to help you mark the scallops or you can use a plate or lid from your kitchen. (See page 127 for instruction on marking the scallop edge.) Baste by hand or machine (with a walking foot) along the marked scalloped edge. ***Do not cut*** on this line yet!

Prepare the bias binding cut 1¼" wide from the solid lavender fabric. Sew together with diagonal seams pressed open. Sew to the quilt with a ¼" seam allowance, stopping to pivot at the inside corners. (See page 128 for instruction on binding a curved edge.) When the binding is sewn on, trim the excess batting and backing to ¼". Turn the binding to the back side of the quilt and stitch down by hand.

Sign and date the quilt for the special lady in your life!

Template
for
Lavender Ladies

Vintage top, hand quilted by author.

Confetti

Confetti

Small fans twirl across the surface of this quilt. The cheerful colors of red and bright yellow make the fans sparkle with energy and excitement! Purchased as a quilt top disaster, it now has a new life. The original top (in a completely different setting) did not lie flat enough to quilt, and the seams were inches apart in meeting. I took the blocks apart, thinking I could simply square the blocks to the same size, but found that many of the blocks did not even resemble squares! The white background fabric was stained, spotted and needed to be replaced, so all the fans were removed from their blocks and were re-appliquéd to new squares of fabric. The fans varied in size and in the number of blades – from five to seven! Obviously, the original maker did not have an accurate template. However, once the quilt top was put together, the varied sizes of the fans was not noticeable. A small red triangle was sewn on the opposite corner of the fan blocks to add an extra note of interest. At the edge of the quilt, those triangles made an interesting "notch" which was repeated on the edge of the quilt.

In spite of all the unexpected problems this quilt posed, I thoroughly enjoyed working on it and hope you will, too. Don't be put off by the number of blocks – with the Easy Dresden tool you can make them accurately the first time.

Quilt shown: (78" x 87"), 4½" blocks, 16 x 18 setting
Lap size: 51" x 60", 10 x 12 setting
(Directions for **smaller** size given in parentheses)

Tool Requirements

Easy Dresden (optional)
Large Square

Fabric Requirements

White: 5¼ yd. (2¼ yd.)
Red solid: 2½ yd. (2 yd.) (includes binding)
Bright yellow solid: 1¼ yd. (⅔ yd.)
Variety of prints: 3½ yd. (1½ yd.) total
   OR ⅞ yd. (⅓ yd.) each of 5 different prints
Backing: 5¼ yd. (3¼ yd.)

Cutting Directions

From	Cut	To Yield
White	36(15) – 5" strips	288(120) 5" squares
Red	12(6) – 1½" strips	320(140) 1½" squares
	18(14) – 1¾" strips	Inner and Outer borders
Variety of prints	2½" strips	1,280(500) wedges cut with Easy Dresden or template page 109
Bright yellow	13(5) – 2" strips	256(100) squares
	9(7) – 1" strips	Middle border

Block Assembly

Note: You can make the blocks as shown in the photo or see page 126 for another option of fans with folded points.

Sew five wedges together to make a fan. If making a smooth edge, turn under the top edge ¼" and press. Baste in place in the corner of a white square.

TIP: To machine baste, set your sewing machine at the longest stitch and stitch ½" from the top edge, down one side and about ½" from the bottom curve of the fan.

Repeat to make 256(100) fan blocks.

Stitch the top curve of the fans in place by hand using a neutral thread and a blind hem stitch.

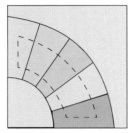

Basting lines

TIP: Beige silk thread is wonderful for this type of appliqué. The thread color blends with any fabric.

Or, use a tiny zigzag or blind hem stitch for machine appliqué. Other options include buttonhole stitching by hand or machine with black thread or with black pearl cotton (#8 for hand stitching), or machine stitch rick-rack over the finished top edge.

Make freezer paper templates for the fan base from the template given on page 109.

TIP: You can re-use the template several times.

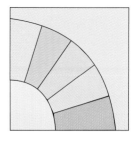

Iron the template to the wrong side of the yellow squares, fitting the corner of the template into the corner of the square. Add a scant ¼" seam allowance to the curved edge only as you are cutting out the shapes. Finger press or, with a warm iron, press the curved edge around the freezer paper template. Stitch the fan base in place by hand or machine. Remove the freezer paper before or after stitching. Remove the basting thread.

At this point you can trim away some of the white background behind the fan and the fan base. This will make it easier to needle for hand quilting. If machine quilting, you can leave the extra fabric behind the fans for added stability.

On the wrong side of each of the red squares, mark a diagonal line. On the corner opposite of the fan base, place a red square as shown. Sew on the marked line. Trim off the excess fabric, leaving a ¼" seam allowance. Press the seam toward the red triangle. Repeat for each of the blocks.

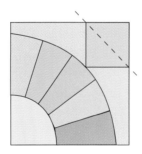 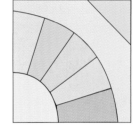

On the remaining 32(20) plain white blocks, add a red square in opposite corners.

Row A Make 2

Row B Make 16

Assembling the Quilt

For the top and bottom A rows, sew together 8(5) fan blocks alternated with 8(5) plain blocks. Press toward the plain blocks.

Make 16(10) B rows as shown. Press as directed. Sew the rows together. Referring to the photo, begin with the top A row, then a B row, followed by a B row reversed. Repeat B and B reversed rows and end with an A row reversed. Press the seams all one direction.

Borders

To make it easier to add the multiple borders, they are first pieced together – red-yellow-red in extra long border lengths, then sewn to the quilt and the corners are mitered. Piece together border lengths longer than needed. Measure, mark, and pin the borders to the quilt. Sew the borders to the quilt beginning and ending ¼" in from each corner. Miter the corners as shown on page 20.

Finishing the Quilt

Mark any quilting designs, then layer, baste, and quilt. The quilt shown was hand-quilted in the ditch between each of the fan wedges, around the base of the fan and at the top curve of the fan. Two more echo lines were quilted following that top curve. The same fan shape was quilted in the plain blocks around the edge of the quilt. The border was quilted ¼" from each of the seams in the red borders only.

Binding

Before binding, mark the notch (pattern given on page 109) at the edges directly above the point where the quilt top is notched. Hand or machine baste (using a walking foot) a scant ¼" from the edge of the quilt, and following the marked notches. **Do not trim** this edge yet!

Cut bias binding strips 1¼" wide from remaining red solid fabric. Join the binding strips with diagonal seams pressed open. Sew to the quilt with a ¼" seam following the directions on page 128 for binding a curved edge. Trim the excess batting and a backing, turn the binding to the back side of the quilt and stitch down by hand.

Sign and date your cheerful masterpiece!

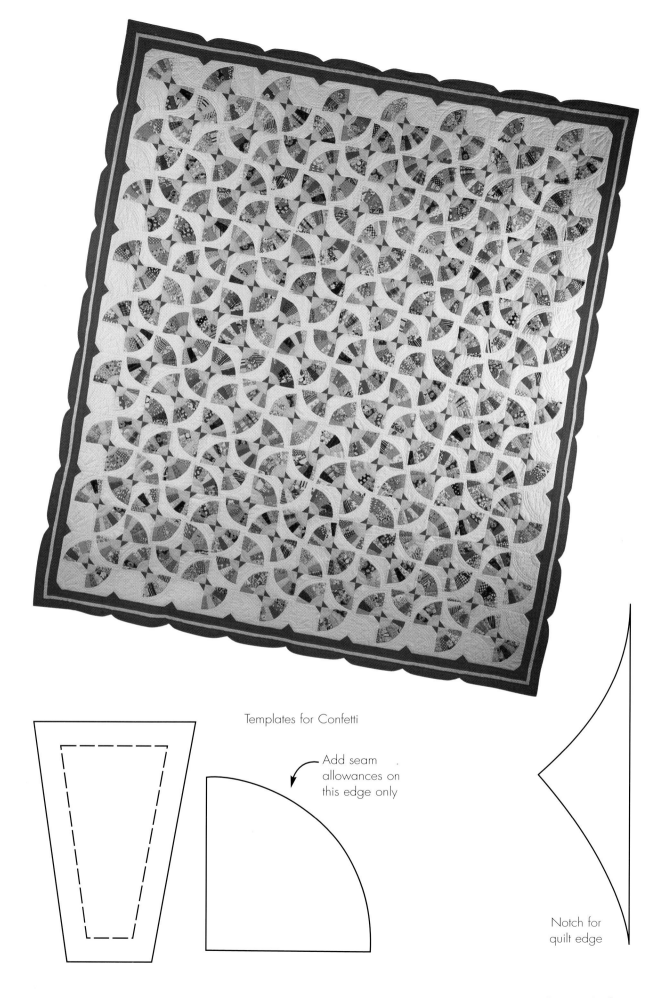

Templates for Confetti

Add seam
allowances on
this edge only

Notch for
quilt edge

Flowers pieced by Grandma Becker, set together and hand-quilted by author.

Grandmother's Flower Garden

Grandma Becker was my husband's grandmother. I never knew her, but she was well known and loved for her sewing skills and her willingness to help others. When she passed away, she left a box of pieced flowers on her treadle sewing machine. The box was marked "For Emily" (my mother-in-law). Although my mother-in-law sewed, she had never pieced quilts and didn't know how to set the flowers together. As *Grandmother's Flower Garden* is one of my favorite patterns of all times, I offered to finish the quilt for her. I saw this unusual setting on an antique quilt, and found that piecing the flowers together in vertical rows was much easier than the typical setting where the flowers are offset.

Hexagon quilts are very old, but before 1920 we don't see them pieced as flower units surrounded by a path. The pastel dressmaking scraps of the '30s were ideal for piecing *Grandmother's Flower Garden*.

It is possible to machine piece this quilt, but you may find it easier to piece by hand. Put the pieces for one flower in a baggie with thread, needle and thread snips, and you have a portable project to take along whenever you have a few minutes to piece. In no time at all you will have the flowers pieced, and can begin setting them together by rows. I am currently piecing my own vintage *Grandmother's Flower Garden*. My husband came home from an auction and told me he had purchased an antique quilt. He handed me a shoebox filled with hundreds of hexagons and quipped, "Some assembly required!"

Wilhelmina Maria Sophia Schwanz-Becker

Fabric Requirements

White: 4 yd.(8 yd.)
Green solid: 1¼ yd.(2¼ yd.)
Variety of solids: 2 yd. total(3½ yd. total)
Variety of prints: 4 yd. total(7 yd. total)
Backing: 4 yd.(8 yd.)

Cutting Directions

Each flower consists of a center (usually yellow), a ring of 6 solid colored hexagons followed by a ring of 12 print hexagons. The flowers are encircled and connected by the "path" which can be any solid color or white. The 4-hexagon unit that fits between the rows can also be any color, contrasting to the path or the same as the path.

From	Cut
White (or yellow)	63(132) hexagons for the flower center (can be white or another color)
Variety of solids	6 hexagons for each flower
Variety of prints	12 hexagons for each flower
White (or another solid)	856(1,772) hexagons for path
Green solid	228(500) hexagons for 4-hexagon units and 3-hexagon units

TIP:

The hexagon template measures 2¼" tall. Cut strips that measurement, then cut hexagons from that strip. By cutting the strips first, you have cut two of the six edges of the hexagon. You will be able to cut approximately 16 hexagons from each 42" strip. The hexagon template is given on page 114.

Assembling the Blocks and Quilt Top

You can piece the flower blocks with the English paper piecing method, or use traditional hand piecing. For the English paper piecing method, you need to cut paper templates the *finished* size of the template. Baste the seam allowances of the larger fabric hexagons over the paper template. The pieces are then joined with a whipstitch. The basting and paper is removed before quilting. This yields very accurate results, but is more time-consuming to do.

You also can piece the hexagons together by hand either eyeballing the seam allowance or marking it lightly with pencil on the wrong side. Sew the hexagons together by hand, using a running stitch, from *seam allowance to seam allowance*, never edge to edge, as *all* the seams are set-in seams.

Start with the flower center; add the solid-colored pieces around the center. Add the ring of print fab-

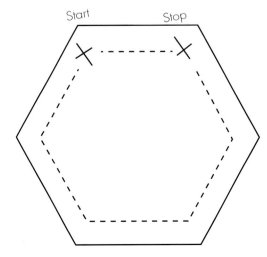

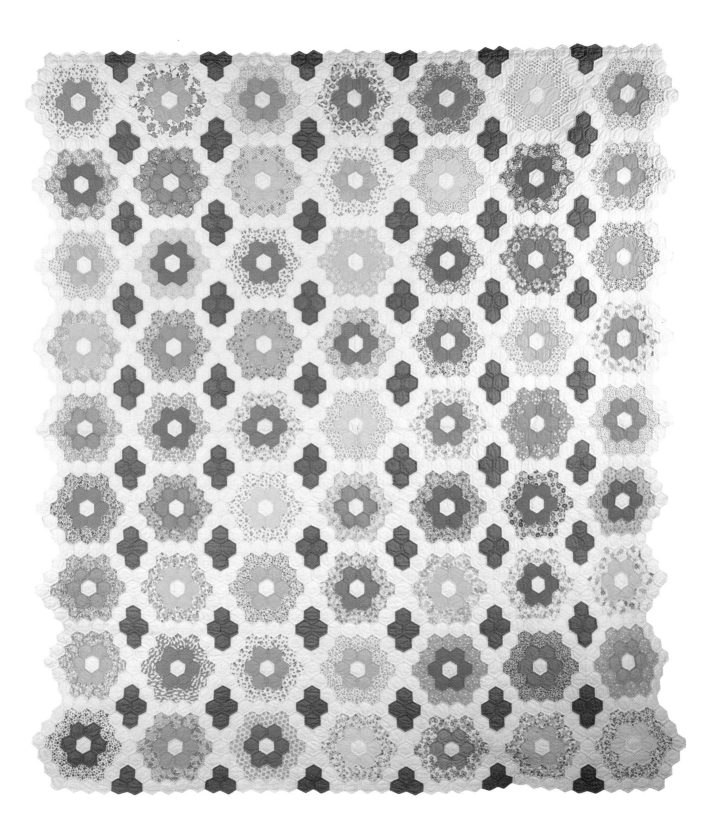

ric last to complete the flower. When the flowers are completed, they can be joined with the white hexagons in long rows, sharing the white path between the flowers.

Note that the rows share the white hexagons at the widest point of the flowers, so on every other row that hexagon needs to be left off. See illustration below.

Grandmother's Flower Garden template

Piece the four-hexagon units to add between the rows. At the top and bottom a three-hexagon unit is substituted for the four-hexagon unit.

The top and bottom edges end straight, and the sides end with a scalloped edge, which looks very pretty on a bed.

Finishing the Quilt

The quilt looks best when quilted ¼" inside of each hexagon. Layer, baste, and quilt. If using Option 3, below, do not quilt the outermost hexagons until after the edge has been finished.

The edge finish on a *Grandmother's Flower Garden* always poses a problem. There are several different solutions:

1. Appliqué a solid colored border to the quilt edge, so you end up with straight sides, which can be easily bound.

2. Trim the edges straight and bind as you would normally.

3. Trim the backing even with the quilt top pieces, following the shape of the hexagons. Trim the batting slightly smaller than the quilt top, following the shape of the hexagons on the edge as before. Turn the quilt top and backing edges under $^{1}/_{4}$" to the inside and whipstitch together. When the edge is completed, go back and quilt around each of the edge hexagons. This option preserves the unique edge of the pieces and is not difficult to do.

Sign and date your very special quilt.

Hand appliquéd and hand quilted by Gay Bomers.

Sunbonnet Sue

S unbonnet Sue is a pattern synonymous with the '30s era, but the roots of the design actually go back to the redwork designs of the late 1880s. Kate Greenway figures were popular for redwork and have some similarity to Sunbonnet Sue. Today we credit Bertha Corbett for adapting the redwork designs into the Sunbonnet Sue patterns we recognize today. There are many different "Sue" designs available, some quite simple. This wonderful Sue design comes from a pattern published by the Kansas City Star newspaper in 1930, designed by Eveline Foland, a free-lance designer.

My friend Gay Bomers hand appliquéd and hand quilted this special quilt using vintage and new fabrics. This would be an ideal place to showcase some vintage feedsack fabrics if you have them! Make it for that special new baby girl in the size shown, or choose the larger twin size for an older child.

Tool Requirements

Large Square
Easy Scallop (optional)

Fabric Requirements

White: 1¾ yd.(5 yd.)
Rose solid: 1¼ yd.(2⅔ yd.)
Variety of prints: 7" square for each dress, smaller pieces for bonnet, shoes, pantaloons, flowers
Green solid: small piece for leaves(⅛ yd.)
Backing: 2½ yd.(5 yd.)

Additional Requirements

Freezer paper or fusible web for appliqué
Black embroidery floss or #8 pearl cotton

Cutting Directions

From	Cut	To Yield
White	3(12) – 9" strips	9(36) – 9" x 11" rectangles
	1(4) – 2½" strips	16(49) 2½" squares
	5(9) – 3¾" strips	Inside border*
	5(9) – 2¼" strips	Binding
Rose solid	3(11) – 2½" strips	12(42) – 2½" x 8½" sashes
	3(11) – 2½" strips	12(42) 2½" x 10½" sashes
	5(9) – 3½" strips	Outer border

You may choose to cut 4-3¾" borders first lengthwise to avoid piecing them.

Appliquéing the Blocks

Trace all the pieces onto the dull side of freezer paper (See page 19 for using fusible web.) For the freezer paper method, cut out the shapes on the marked lines. Iron to the wrong side of the fabric chosen for the appliqué. Cut out, adding a scant ¼". Press the edges of the fabric around the freezer paper. Remove the freezer paper.

Crease the white rectangle from both sides to mark the center. Use those lines to help you position the shapes on the block. Layer in the correct order, then baste in place. You can choose to do hand or machine appliqué, buttonhole stitch or as shown in the example, use a running stitch in black embroidery floss or pearl cotton close to the edges to hold the pieces in place.

Note: If you stitch a running stitch close to the edges of the turned-under appliqués, you do not need to appliqué them down first.

Embroider the details on the bonnet, the pantaloons, and the flower stem and flower center (buttons could also be used for the flower centers). Make 9(36) blocks. When the blocks are finished, *trim evenly to measure 8½" x 10½".*

Assembling the Quilt

Join 3(6) blocks and 4(7) 2½" x 10½" rose solid sashes to make a row. Press seams toward the sashing. Make 3(6) rows of blocks and sashes.

Assemble 4(7) rows with 4(7) white cornerstones and 3(6) 2½" x 8½" rose solid sashes.

Sunbonnet Sue

Press seams toward the sashing.

Join the block rows and sashing rows. Press the seams toward the sashing rows.

Borders

Cut (and piece if necessary) four borders from both of the fabrics *longer* than needed. Baste the white border on top of the rose border, with 1½" of the rose fabric extending beyond the white border.

Trim two borders to the width of the quilt. Sew to the top and bottom of the quilt. Press the seams toward the borders. (See page 19 for instruction on adding borders.)

Trim the remaining two borders to the length of the quilt. Sew to the sides. Press the seams toward the borders.

Using Easy Scallop or a dish or plate in your kitchen of the right diameter, mark 4" scallops on the white border, rounding the corners. Cut on the marked line, then turn the edges under ¼" and appliqué down by hand or machine. If the rose fabric shadows through, trim away, leaving a scant ¼" seam allowance.

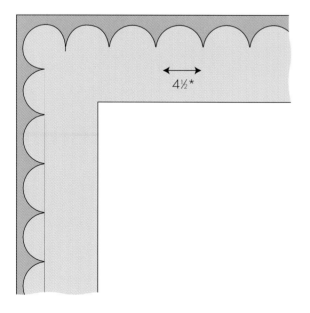

4½"

Finishing the Quilt

Mark any quilting designs on the quilt top. Layer, baste, and quilt. The quilt shown was hand quilted around the appliqué shapes and a diagonal line was quilted 1" apart in each of the blocks. A cable design was quilted in the sashings and cornerstones. The scalloped edge was quilted on both sides of the seam lines.

Binding

Before binding, hand or machine baste (with a walking foot) a scant ¼" from the edge of the quilt. This will keep the layers from shifting when the binding is sewn on.

Prepare the binding (see page 21 for instruction on binding) and sew to the quilt with a ¼" seam. Trim off excess batting and backing, and turn the binding to the wrong side. Stitch down by hand.

Sign and date your special quilt!

Eveline Roland

clip and save.

Here comes "Sunbonnet Sue" to surely down upon your bed quilt patch and settle herself on dressing scarf or form the motif quaint little boudoir pillow. Her may be either flowered or fabric and her cunning pant- a piece of embroidery or a of lace. Her bonnet, arm and foot can be of any harmonizing color, to be determined by the fabric chosen for the dress.

The little figure is appliqued on a block 9x11 inches and stripped together with bands of the solid fabric two inches wide. The flower may be used in each corner, which will be a 2-inch square of the same material as used for a background. Lay piece of tissue paper over "Sue" trace. Then cut out for pattern. simple running stitch may be after all edges have been turne This is a nice patch for little who are just learning to sew comparatively simple, yet charm. Allow for seams.

(Copyright 1930 by the Kaiser

Vintage top hand quilted by author.

Sunny Side Up

A perennial favorite – the Dresden Plate – first appeared around 1930, and was a popular pattern of its time, and continues to be to this day. A variation of the Dresden Plate is Grandmother's Fan (example on page 90). A Dresden Plate can have any number of wedges and the edges may be rounded or pointed. The center can be large or small, a circle appliquéd over the top or the center left open. Each block could have the same prints in the same locations or each block could have a variety of prints – your choice!

Usually the blocks are set next to one another; occasionally with sashing, and sometimes even a four-leaf clover shape is appliquéd where four blocks meet. This vintage quilt is made extra-special with the addition of the yellow and white ice cream cone border.

You can reproduce the quilt exactly as shown using the templates on page 122, or you can use the Easy Dresden tool to rotary cut the wedges, giving you 20 wedges instead of 14, and a larger center. Cut the edges rounded and appliqué them to the block, or use an optional method of making pointed corners with pre-finished points that don't even need to be appliquéd in place! See page 126 for instruction on making those folded points.

Tool Requirements

Large Square
Easy Dresden (optional)

Fabric Requirements

White: 5 yd.(7½ yd.)
Yellow solid: 2½ yd.(2¾ yd.) (includes bias binding)
Variety of prints: ¼ yd.(⅜ yd.) of at least 20 prints or 3½ yd.(5½ yd.) total **if using Easy Dresden**
OR: Variety of prints: ⅓ yd. (⅝) of at least 14 prints or 3¾ (5¾) total if using template
Backing: 4¾ yd.(8 yd.)

Cutting Directions

From	Cut	To Yield
White	12(19) – 12½" strips	36(56) – 12½" squares
	5(7) – 3¾" strips	116(150) of Template A for border***
		8 Template B for border corners
Assorted prints	4" strips	720(1120) wedges if using Easy Dresden*
Yellow solid:		36(56) center circles**
	7(8) – 4⅜" strips	124(158) of Template B for border***

*If not using Easy Dresden, see page 122 for template. Cut 504(784).
**Use the circle template from the Easy Dresden package for the center circle if using the tool. See page 122 if using the template for the plates.
*** See page 122 for templates A and B for the ice cream cone border.

Block Assembly

If you are using the Easy Dresden method and making the folded point wedges, see page 126 in the Tool Tutorial for instruction.

Join 20 wedges for each of 36(56) plates. Crease the background squares in half from both directions. Using the creases for orientation, center and baste the plates on the blocks. You can stitch the outside edges down by hand or machine, appliqué with decorative black buttonhole stitch, or just fasten the blocks in place with the quilting later if you have made the folded points.

If you are using the template on page 122, baste all the rounded edges under ¼" by hand before joining the wedges. Join 14 wedges (see stitching directions for Easy Dresden page 127) with the thread ends hidden below the edge of the block. Baste, then appliqué the plates by hand or machine onto the blocks.

Make a circle template out of freezer paper at the finished size. Cut out and iron to the wrong side of the fabric chosen for the centers. Cut out the circles, adding a scant ¼" seam allowance. Finger press or, with an iron, press the fabric edges around the circle. Appliqué in place, removing the freezer paper before finishing.

At this point, you can trim away some of the background fabric if you choose.

TIP: An optional appliqué method would be to slip the fabric circle under the plate and turn the edges of the plate in ¼". Stitch down by hand or machine.

Assembling the Quilt

Join the blocks in 6(8) rows of 6(7) blocks. Press the seams in each row in alternating directions so the seams will butt up. Sew the rows together. Press the seams all one direction.

Borders

Join 29(34) white wedges cut from Template A, below, with 31(36) solid-yellow wedges cut from Template B, below. Use two white Template B pieces at both ends. Make four borders the same.

For the larger quilt cut 34 white wedges and 41 yellow wedges for the longer sides.

Sew borders to opposite sides of the quilt. Press.

Note: If the borders don't fit quite right, adjust the seams as needed in several of the wedges.

Sew the remaining borders to the quilt sides, joining the border wedges at the corners before finishing the seams that attach the borders.

Finishing the Quilt

Mark any quilting designs on the quilt top. Layer, baste, and quilt. The quilt shown was hand-quilted ¼" from the seams in each of the wedges and around the circle in the center. Quilt in concentric circles following the outside curves of the plates. Where four blocks meet, stitch a simple four-lobed

design to fill up that area. The ice cream cones in the border were quilted ¼" from each seam.

Binding

Cut bias strips from yellow solid 1¼" wide. Join with diagonal seams pressed open. Before sewing the binding, hand or machine baste a scant ¼" from the edge of the quilt. Stitch the binding to the right side of the quilt using a ¼" seam allowance and pivoting with the needle down and pressure foot up at the midpoint of the white triangles in the border. Ease the binding around the curved edges. Trim any excess batting and backing. Turn the binding to the back of the quilt, turn it under ¼" and stitch in place by hand on the back side. (See page 128 for binding a curved edge.)

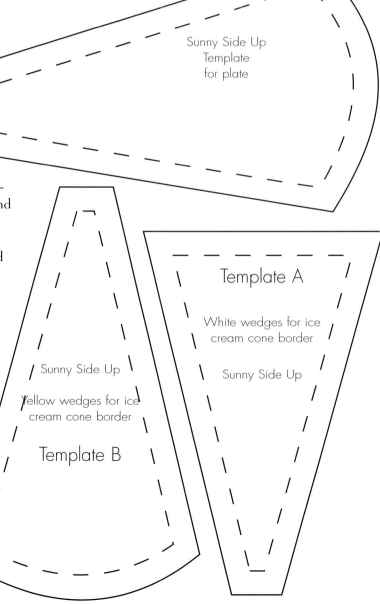

Sunny Side Up
Template
for plate

Template A

White wedges for ice cream cone border

Sunny Side Up

Sunny Side Up

Yellow wedges for ice cream cone border

Template B

Sunny Side Up
Template
Plate Center
(finished size)

Sunny Side Up

Tool Tutorial

Tri-Recs™ Tools

To cut Tri triangles, lay the tool on the strip with the top flat edge at the top of the strip, and a line on the tool aligned with the bottom of the strip. Cut on both sides of the triangle. The patterns will tell you what size strip to cut—always ½" larger than the finished size.

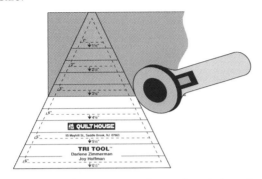

For the second cut, rotate the tool so it is pointing down. Align as before and cut.

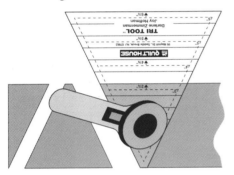

To cut Recs triangles, cut the same size strip as for the large triangles. Leave the strip folded and you will automatically cut pairs of Recs triangles. Align the tool with the flat top edge at the top of the strip, and a line on the tool aligned with the bottom of the strip. Cut on the angled edge, then swing around and nip off the "magic angle" at the top. This

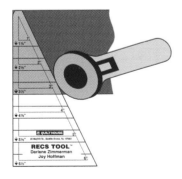

needs to be cut accurately, as it is your alignment guide when sewing the pieces together.

For the second cut, rotate the tool so it is point-

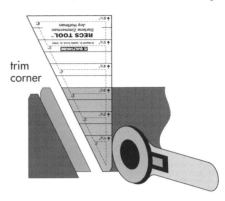

ing down. Align as before and cut, then swing back and trim off the "magic angle."

Together the two tools cut the shapes for making a triangle within a square. Lay out the pieces as shown to form a square.

Fit the Recs triangle into the corner of the large triangle. Note how the "magic angle" will fit right

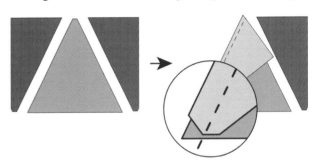

into the corner as shown. Yes, the pieces look odd at this point, but they will be right when sewn!

Piecing Rectangles

Place two Recs triangles right sides together, fitting the "magic angle" into the corner as shown. Stitch and press toward the darker fabric.

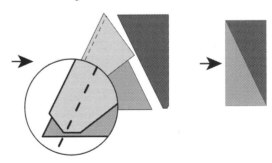

Easy Angle™

This tool comes in two different sizes, 4½" and 6½". You may use either one for the projects in this book. Easy Angle allows you to cut triangle squares from the same size strip as for squares. You only need to add a ½" seam allowance when using Easy Angle (instead of that nasty ⅞" you add when cutting squares, then cutting on the diagonal).

To use the tool most efficiently, layer the fabric strips you are using for your triangle squares right sides together, then cut with Easy Angle. They will then be ready to chain-sew.

Before making the first cut, trim off the selvages. Then align the top flat edge of the tool at the top of the strip, matching a line on the tool with the bottom edge of the strip. Cut on the diagonal edge.

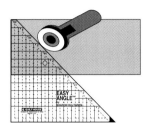

To make the second cut, rotate the tool so the flat edge is aligned at the bottom of the strip, and a line on the tool is aligned with the top of the strip. Cut again.

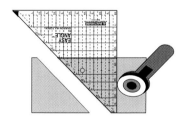

Continue in this manner down the strip. Chain-sew the triangles on the longest edge. Press toward the darkest fabric and trim dog-ears.

Note: If you choose not to use Easy Angle in the projects, you will need to add ⅞" to all the finished sizes of the units. Then cut a strip that width. For example, instead of cutting a 2½" strip to yield ½" triangle squares, cut a 2⅞" strip instead. Then cut squares, and cut the squares once on the diagonal.

Companion Angle™

Companion Angle allows you to cut quarter-square triangles—or triangles with the longest edge on the straight of grain. A common use for this type

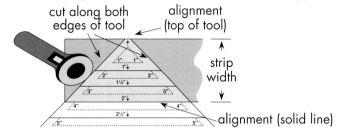

of triangle is the "goose" in flying geese.

To cut with Companion Angle, align the top flat point of the tool with the top edge of the strip. A line on the tool should align with the bottom of the

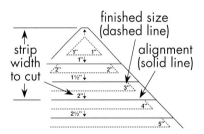

strip. Cut on both sides of the tool.

For the next cut, rotate the tool so the point of the tool is at the bottom of the strip, and a line on the tool is aligned with the bottom of the strip. Cut again.

Continue in this manner down the strip of fabric.

Note: If not using Companion Angle, you will need to add 1¼" to the finished size of the base of the triangle you are cutting. Cut a square that size, then cut it twice on the diagonal to yield 4

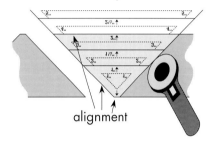

triangles. For example, the "goose" you are cutting will finish to 3" across the base. Add 1¼" + 3" = 4¼". Cut a 4¼" square, then cut twice to yield 4 triangles.

Easy EIGHT™

Easy Eight allows you to cut diamonds of various sizes without a template. Use the tool as a ruler to cut the strip for the size diamond you have chosen.

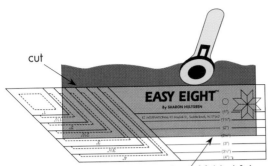

cut

line up squared edge of folded fabric on line corresponding to diamond size

Slide the tool on the end of the strip, trimming off the first angle.

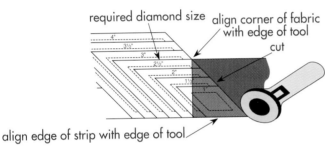

required diamond size

align corner of fabric with edge of tool

cut

align edge of strip with edge of tool

Slide the tool further along the strip until the entire diamond is filled up. Cut again.
Continue in this manner down the strip.

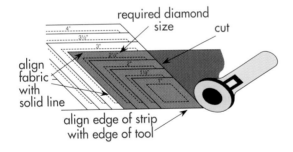

required diamond size

cut

align fabric with solid line

align edge of strip with edge of tool

All these tools can be found at your local quilt, craft or fabric store. If you cannot find them locally, you may call (800) 660-0415 to order from EZ Quilting by Wrights.

Easy Dresden™

The tool would cut wedges from a strip of fabric in this manner.

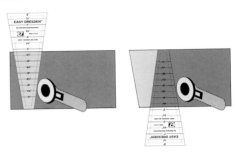

FINISHING THE EDGES

The top edge of the completed circle can be turned under ¼" in a smooth curve, or the top of each wedge can be curved by using the template given in the package to recut the tops of the wedges after they've been cut from the fabric strip.

To make finished points on the top of each wedge, fold the top edges right sides together and using a short stitch length, sew a ¼" seam. Clip the folded corner at an angle, turn the point and press with the seam centered on the wedge, as seen below.

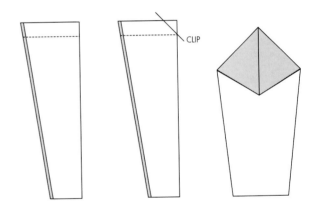

CLIP

JOINING THE WEDGES

Use an exact ¼" seam when sewing the wedges together. Handle all the pieces gently, as they have bias edges. Press the seams all one direction around the circle or quarter circle. You may do this as you sew each piece, or sew the entire Dresden Plate or Fan together before pressing. (NOTE: Use a dry iron so the circle is not stretched out of round.)

If you have sewn the top seam of the wedges to make a point, join the wedges by starting the stitching ¼" from the top edge, backstitch to the top edge, then continue stitching the rest of the seam.

This will prevent your wedges pulling apart, and the thread ends will be hidden underneath.

If making rounded tops on the wedges, start

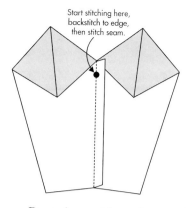

Start stitching here, backstitch to edge, then stitch seam.

stitching ¼" from the top edge to allow for turn-under.

FINISHING

Twenty wedges are joined for one Dresden Plate. Fold the background square in fourths, and use the creased lines to center the Dresden Plate. Baste in position, then applique by hand or machine. A center is usually appliqued last in the center of the plate, or the inside edges can just be turned under and appliqued in place.

Five wedges make up a Grandmother's Fan or other variation of the fan. When the fan wedges are joined, applique them to a corner of a square, adding the quarter circle last.

The background fabric can be trimmed away from underneath the fan or plate, or it can be left in for stabilization.

Easy Tri-Mate™

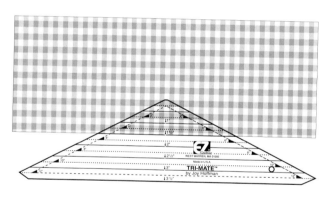

The Tri-Mate tools works with the Tri-Recs tools to make long flat flying geese units or elongated hourglass units.

To make:  Cut one TRI-MATE™, cut 2 Recs Triangles.

To make: Cut two TRI-MATES™, cut 2 Tri Triangles.

The measurements on the outer edge of the tool give you the finished base measurement ranging from 2" - 12". You can actually see the finished size in the dashed lines, and the solid lines are your "cutting" lines. The center marking on the tool will tell you what size strip to cut for the size triangle you have chosen.

Cut a strip to the desired width, then lay the tool on the strip and cut on both sides of the tool to make a triangle. For the second cut you will reverse the tool and cut again. After the triangles are cut, go back and align the base of the tool on the cut triangles and trim off both corners to make alignment easier when sewing.

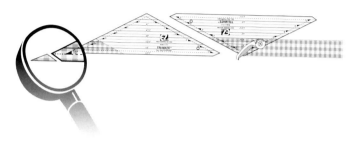

Easy Scallop™
MEASURING:

Measure the length of the border.

Choose desired *number* of scallops. Divide the border length by that number. This will give you scallop *size*. *Border length divided by number of scallops=scallop size.* Round the answer to the nearest quarter inch. Set the Easy Scallop™ tool at that measurement you have chosen.

MARKING:

To mark a rounded corner, begin at one corner and mark a full scallop. Mark from both ends toward the center, so if any adustments need to be made, you can make them in the center. (Diagram A) To mark a pointed corner, begin at one corner and mark a half scallop, leaving the corner square. Again, mark from both ends toward the center. (Diagram B)

Diagram A

X START HERE FOR ROUNDED CORNER

Diagram B

X START HERE FOR POINTED CORNER

BINDING:

Do not cut on the marked line!

Quilt, then before binding, hand-baste along the

marked scallop line. This will keep the layers from shifting when the binding is sewn on.

A bias binding is a must for binding curved edges. Cut your binding strips at a 45 degree angle, and join with diagonal seams pressed open. A single binding cut at 1¼" will finish to ¼". (Diagram C)

Press the beginning edge under ¼". With right sides together and the raw edge of the binding aligned with the marked border, begin stitching a ¼" seam at the top of the scallop.

Stitch to the base of the V, stop with the needle down at that point. Lift the presser foot, pivot the quilt and binding to begin sewing out of the V. Put the presser foot down and sew out of the V, taking care not to stitch any pleats in the binding. (Diagram D)

Continue around the quilt in this manner, **easing** the binding around the curves, not stretching it. Overlap the beginning edge by 1", trim off at an angle.

Trim the seam allowance even with the edge of the binding. Turn the binding to the back side, turn under ¼" and stitch down by hand, covering the stitching line. The inside corners will just fold over upon themselves automatically.

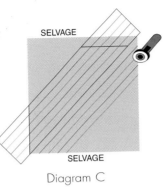

SELVAGE

SELVAGE

Diagram C

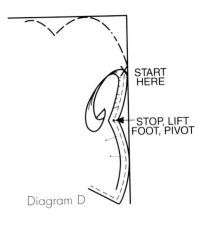

START HERE

STOP, LIFT FOOT, PIVOT

Diagram D

Tools

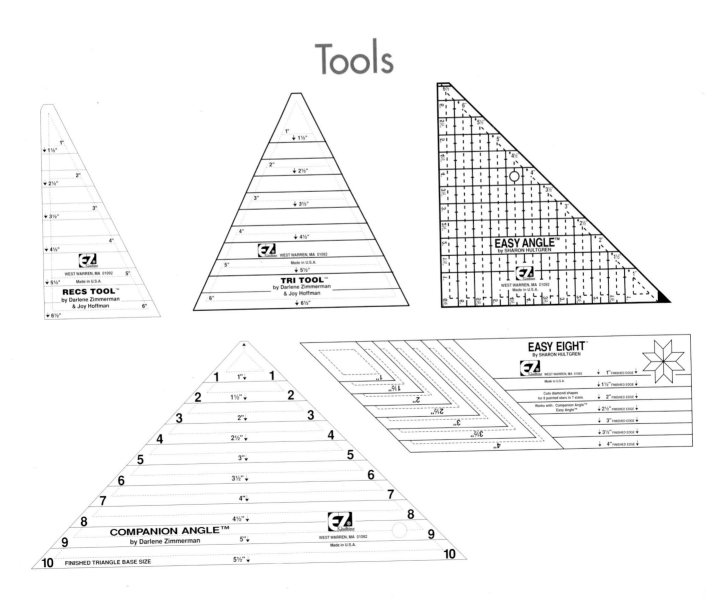